The Speculative Strategist

The Speculative Strategist

High Returns from Controlled Risk Strategies in Stock and Futures Markets

Will Slatyer

McGraw-Hill

New York San Francisco Washington, D.C. Auckland Bogotá
Caracas Lisbon London Madrid Mexico City Milan
Montreal New Delhi San Juan Singapore
Sydney Tokyo Toronto

Library of Congress Cataloging-in-Publication Data

Slatyer, Will.
The speculative strategist : high returns from controlled risk strategies in stock and futures markets / by Will Slatyer.
p. cm.
Includes bibliographical references and index.
ISBN 0-07-058143-6
1. Stocks. 2. Stock exchanges. 3. Futures. 4. Futures market. 5. Risk management. 6. Portfolio management. I. Title.
HG4521.S625 1996
372.63'228—dc20 95-12422
CIP

McGraw-Hill

A Division of The McGraw-Hill Companies

1 2 3 4 5 6 7 8 9 0 DOC/DOC 9 0 1 0 9 8 7 6

ISBN 0-07-058143-6

The sponsoring editor for this book was David Conti, the editing supervisor was Patricia V. Amoroso, and the production supervisor was Suzanne Kapcavage. It was set in Palatino by Victoria Khavkina of McGraw-Hill's Professional Book Group composition unit.

Printed and bound by R. R. Donnelley & Sons Company.

This book is printed on recycled, acid-free paper containing a minimum of 50% recycled de-inked fiber.

Contents

Preface

I have written *The Speculative Strategist* for the individual speculator in futures and stocks who wishes to structure a sound, disciplined method of making money for themselves and their loved ones from the markets. Traders, from professional to novice, will gain a sense of the strategic qualities and resources needed to profit continually in fast-moving modern speculative markets. By many measures, the majority of today's markets are speculative.

The market novice will find the early chapters easy to read and understand but might find details of technical analysis later in the book slightly confusing. I make no apology for this. The principles I have outlined should enable novice trading to become profitable in a short time. However, those who have no prior knowledge of technical analysis will need to seek further education in this extremely important facet of financial analysis before they can formulate their own technical plans. Technical analysis requires some study before one can become proficient, but is well worth the effort. I hope that I have succeeded in encouraging this study.

Professional traders might find the pirate and privateer allegory somewhat colorful for a description of what are supposedly standard trading principles of fund management. They might even find some of their trading values questioned. This is necessary. Many traders concentrate almost completely on technological toys, often at the expense of sound principle. I have tried to demonstrate principles that in recent years might have gone out of fashion, but which are still relevant. The professional technical analyst might also question my use of simple techniques, but they work. All the details are produced which allow independent testing of these techniques. Technological breakthroughs in recent years have produced more complicated instant computerized techniques, but do not appear to have produced the same quantum leap in profits of many managed funds. The systems which I have outlined in this book are admittedly simple in concept, but can be filtered through one's own values to produce a personal trading plan of the desired complexity.

I have been monitoring international futures, foreign exchange, and interest rate markets for more than thirty years, mainly from the point of view of a risk manager. Even the professional traders reading this book may have forgotten the principles of structured risk management, which seemed to fade around 1986, about the time when I commenced tracking international stock markets for inclusion in a conservative investment model. To my risk management principles I then added a rule that also may have been neglected in recent years: Hedge in adverse circumstances, but do not quit an investment until a better alternative has been established.

Principles provide a sound base for timely action in the markets, and sound techniques are needed for that action. In the 1960s I had become intrigued with one of the simplest forms of technical analysis—moving averages. The advent of software for the personal computer in the 1980s greatly increased the interest in various forms of technical analysis. Most professional traders moved on to new and exciting methods of trading that the computer made possible, and of which neural network programs are but the latest.

Rather than use each new technical tool that became available, I used the new computer technology to improve the simple moving-average technique which I had earlier developed by hand-held calculator. The system and software which I developed was able to provide risk management advice superior to that offered by many major institutions. I was surprised to learn that my international investment model, developed for the chairman of one of my risk management clients, had, with 20% per annum noncumulative returns, proven more profitable than the methods of established European fund managers. Apart from a few personal, often ill-timed, bursts, I neglected short-term speculation.

I would like to credit the founder of Computrac, Tim Slater, with stimulating my serious examination of speculation and for planting the seeds for this book. In 1993, Tim invited me to make a presentation to TAG XV, the annual seminar of the Technical Analysis Group. This group was originally the driving force behind the world's first technical analysis personal computer software company, Computrac. Tim knew of my work in structured financial risk management, but told me that seminar delegates would be much more interested in speculative techniques.

My presentation to TAG XV was purposefully quite technical because, as an Australian without day-to-day contact with U.S. nonprofessionals, I believed that American traders were much more advanced than those "Down Under." I have since spoken to traders in New Zealand, England, Holland, and Japan as well as the United States, and now believe that no one corner of the globe has the edge in technical trading strategy. Tim's later comments that my ideas were maybe a little sophisticated for a seminar audience which included many novices led me to look for an allegory to describe the whole concept of speculation in a simpler form. The technical strategy which I presented in 1993 forms the basis of the Woodes Rogers strategy described in this book.

I was already working on a financial risk-management philosophy that followed many sound principles of war, and which will form the basis of coming books. Simply put, I believe that market capitalism of the twentieth century is merely a socially acceptable form of the warfare that humans have practiced for millennia, in which money flows instead of blood. Corporate capitalism was relatively organized, with its own rules of engagement, policy, strategy, and tactics. Speculation, even that of a corporate variety, was apparently considered too chaotic and fast moving to be subject to trading by war game principles.

Then, while researching historical money market principles, I discovered that the founder of the Bank of England, William Paterson, had been a buccaneer in his youth. A buccaneer—a freebooting pirate, similar to Long John Silver from Robert Louis

Stevenson's book *Treasure Island*. I am not quite old enough to have read the original 1883 book, but admit to having read a reprint more than once before I saw the 1950 Disney movie, following which Robert Newton, playing Long John Silver, also appeared in boys' nightmares. Having been involved in several litigation battles with banks as an expert witness, the idea of buccaneers progressing to bankers intrigued me. Further research led me to the speculative metaphor of privateers and pirates.

The idea of looking back into history for role models owes much to the comments of a famous U.S. lawyer and cynic, Clarence Darrow. At the dawn of the twentieth century, Darrow said, "History repeats itself. That's the trouble with history."

In fact the premise of historical repetition is not problematic at all to students of financial markets who have learned that profits can be made from identifying common patterns of market behavior. Traders who analyze the markets to discern patterns of the past are called technical analysts, to differentiate them from those dependent on fundamental analysis of supply and demand.

Technical analysts suggest that actions of all market participants from all over the world are combined to produce the crowd behavior responsible for price trends. Crowd behavior has changed little throughout the ages, so that the actions of the crowd can be forecast to some degree by using crowd psychology. The actions of the relatively uneducated crowd during the South Sea Bubble of 1720 were very similar to those of the more modern computerized crowd in the 1987 stock market mania. Technical analysis is the chart whereby the temperature of the crowd can be monitored to determine the start of likely fevers or frosts. History *is* repetitive, and by forecasting repetitive action, speculative profits can be made.

My concept that speculative activity is best approached with preformed policy and strategy, before applying technical tactics, also owes much to history, and in particular to a 2200-year-old Chinese book *The Art of War*. Like many executives, for many years I used the words "policy," "strategy," and "tactics" interchangeably in boardroom discussions. An English translation of Sun Tsu's *The Art of War*, which I picked up while in transit through Singapore many years ago, made the differences between the meanings of the three terms clear. Also known as *The Art of*

Strategy, the book has formed the basis of many business books in the last decade, so there are a number of translations available for further reading. Keen capitalist warriors might search for a little-known book of the same name by the fifteenth-century strategist Nicholo Machievelli, who is more famous for his book *The Prince*.

Finally, there are many hundreds of people whom I should thank for their influences on this book. My grasp of short-term technical analysis owes much to observations of many market participants, who won and lost in the daily skirmishes with the crowd, so I thank these soldiers who can remain unknown. To authors long dead, and to those very much alive, I express my thanks. In particular I would like to thank the still lively systems guru, Perry Kaufman, for his support.

Will Slatyer

The Speculative Strategist

1

Speculative Philosophy: Privateer or Pirate

The Search for the Secret of Speculative Profits

During my thirty years trading futures and financial markets as a broker and risk manager, I have encountered hundreds of speculators, but those who were consistently profitable could be counted in tens. I have met traders whose intelligence bordered on genius, but who consistently made fundamental errors. Professional traders with large capital and the latest in sophisticated computer programs have made a series of reasonable profits, and then been hit by a huge loss. Novice excitement seekers have always been profitable for commission merchants, because of the uncontrolled urge to always be in the market, trading constantly until their money ran out.

I have known some large losers. One very intelligent man lost a petroleum company because he refused to quit a bear position in a bull market. Another, an international sports hero, tragically took his own life following sharp reverses in the gold market, in which he had also traded clients' funds.

I have known fewer consistent winners. One battling farmer traded a few thousand dollars into the price of a large farming property, and then quit the markets. A young man whom I introduced to the floor in his teens became a local floor trader and made so much money he became bored. He now takes long absences from the floor traveling the world, before again returning to the markets. A good friend, one of the best "gut feel" traders I have known, now is happy to scalp $500–$1000 per day without overnight positions, so that he can leave the floor early to spend time with his children.

A number of large winners have been eulogized in Jack Schwager's books on "market wizards." One must marvel at the success of these men, who appear to have the aptitude of time travelers. Collectively they appear to have the patience of a biblical Job, the policy grasp of Charlemagne, strategies of Merlin, discipline of Julius Caesar, and can operate the technology of NASA with a Midas touch. The ordinary speculator can be inspired by these Wizard winners, but might not be able to apply the examples to their own trading.

My search for the secrets of profitable speculation had to uncover methods which the average professional trader could use or that the dilettante could learn. I had to produce a system for mere mortals, which did not rely on superior natural skills.

The success of the "wizards" proved that speculation could be highly profitable, and I knew from my own risk management operation that systematic trading could be consistently profitable. So why did so many speculators continue to lose?

My conclusion, after much research, was that traders are concentrating their attention on the actual trade, entry and exit, and short-term movement while neglecting the long-term and strategic implications of their trading. Modern technology has allowed us to watch tick-by-tick movement of markets, and accompanying real-time information flows. It is natural that traders focus on the electronic output and use the adrenaline of market action to precipitate trading decisions.

> *If I have been able to see further than other men, it was because I have stood on the shoulders of giants.*
>
> SIR ISAAC NEWTON, 1642–1727

Box 1-1.

The secret which I might have discovered is that this concentration on the near-term activity has been at the expense of long-term planning. At a seminar where I presented technical analysis of the 1994 bond market, I displayed a monthly chart of T-Bonds and the evidence of a major top well before the market collapsed. One fund manager confessed that he had not looked at a monthly chart since he became an active trader. This manager of millions of dollars was so tied up in his short-term trading program that he had forgotten to look at the big picture. Publicized 1994 losses suggest that this man was not alone.

From my early days as a diver with the Royal Australian Navy, I was aware of the tremendous amount of planning and preparation that preceded a successful mission. Modern recreational scuba divers are taught an adage to reduce the incidence of accidents: "Plan your dive. Dive your plan."

Before my Navy team entered the water, we knew distances, tides, currents, targets, defenses, and support. We had trained extensively on the rebreathing diving equipment that left no visible sign of our approach, and which we could adjust automatically by touch in complete darkness. Each member of the team had a defined role, that was known by the other frogmen so that backup could be provided if necessary.

The actual diving of the plan was the exciting key to the overall success of the mission. Without the preparation, the dive might have been even more exciting, but might also have produced an unsuccessful mission. The adrenaline of action was a by-product of the mission, and in fact tended to be downplayed by the senior officers responsible for success.

Should not success be the main purpose of speculation? Should not the excitement of trading be secondary to success? Would this type of thinking from naval history produce a method of trading futures and financial markets which would provide consistent success?

In my mind some techniques of war could be readily applied to the markets. What is capitalism but a socially acceptable form of warfare in which money flows instead of blood? Speculation in financial markets is the riskiest form of capitalism, but no more risky than frogman or commando raids.

If I were to be able to teach this uncovered secret to traders more interested in market action than analysis, I would need an allegory to convince traders to examine a different emphasis. When I studied the art of war looking for an allegory, I found that the thinking preceding a battle had changed little over the centuries. Technology has changed from the arrow to the guided missile, but strategic preparation today is much the same as it was in the days of Alexander the Great.

But my research into the policy of war and the strategy of battles failed to produce the examples I was seeking to demonstrate planning techniques for market speculation. There were examples for corporate activity. In military terms, financial risk management can follow the metaphor of embattled siege mentality, or maybe the planning of highly mobile defense forces trained to attack as well as defend. Investment can be defined as the advance of a well-armed convoy, in which the defense of objectives already captured is at least as important as the gains from fresh advances. And the winning of battles is most often a triumph of the organization of large forces, which could not be reproduced by an individual speculator. The policy and strategy that direct an army appeared to be unsuited to the resources available to the average speculator.

The Art of War

The Art of War was written by a legendary Chinese general, Sun Tsu, somewhere between 551 B.C., the probable birth date of Confucius, and 223 B.C., when the first emperor of the Chin dynasty was proclaimed.

The Art of War can be translated into advice to market strategists:

> Know your enemy, know yourself,
> and your victory shall not be threatened.
> Know the terrain, know the weather
> and your victory shall be complete.

Box 1-2.

Financial Speculation

It next occurred to me that financial speculation might be the embodiment of guerrilla warfare, where highly mobile teams of skilled warriors attacked entrenched positions with the objective of rich rewards. Further study of the history of warfare disabused me of this notion. Guerrilla warfare is basically an ideological war of attrition, aimed at the collapse of a political system. The number of losses and atrocities far outweigh the heroic successes. Even when guerrilla warfare is successful in controlling government, the country has often been debilitated to such a degree that it regains stability only slowly, under leaders not particularly suited to sound governance. Speculation of the guerrilla type has been carried out without lasting success, such as in the attempt to corner the silver market by the Hunt brothers in 1979–1980.

Following further study, now of naval warfare, I finally formed the opinion that modern financial speculation might indeed have its origins in the seventeenth century with the growth of war at sea. Privateering and piracy is a great analogy for financial speculation. Why? Because financial speculation can be seen as a series of fluid attacks on financial markets, using well-financed modern vessels, which can avoid high risk by speed and daring, and can capture rich rewards.

A *successful* financial speculator in the twentieth century will have the best attributes of a *privateer* from the golden age of piracy in the seventeenth and eighteenth centuries. The *least* successful financial speculator will enjoy the excitement and brief rewards of a *pirate,* but will, more often than not, also experience the quick demise of most pirates.

Privateers or Pirates

What is the difference between a privateer and pirate? This is a question that has been asked for millennia, since the introduction of sail to large vessels allowed wide-ranging trade by daring merchant adventurers from the Gulf of Oman. By the ninth century B.C., trading posts had been established in Java, Sumatra, and Siam, and voyages commenced to obtain Chinese silk from Canton.

Cargoes of spice, precious metals and jewels, ivory, and teak en route through Oman to Babylon attracted daring merchant adventurers who became known as "pirates."

The word *pirate* is derived from the Greek *peiran,* meaning "to attempt" or "to attack." The Assyrian king Sennacherib led a naval expedition against seagoing brigands in the seventh century B.C.

The word *privateer* does not appear in the records until the seventeenth century, but as early as 594 B.C. the Laws of Solon in Athens refer to authorized associations of pirates. The authorities of the Greek city-states could not afford a regular navy, so they employed bands of seagoing brigands to fight naval wars on *commissions.* Merchants were authorized to outfit vessels to take reprisals to the estimated value of earlier stolen cargoes.

The continual wars between the feuding nations of England, Spain, France, Portugal, and Holland encouraged monarchs short of cash to allow pirates to attack ships of other nations in the name of patriotism. The name *privateer* came to mean a privately owned and armed vessel *commissioned* by a belligerent state to attack enemy ships, usually vessels of commerce. Crews were not paid by the commissioning government but were entitled to cruise for profit, with crew members receiving portions of the value of any cargo or shipping prizes.

In 1630 Charles I of England licensed Captain Quail of the *Seahorse* to "make purchase in the Red Sea, as well as anywhere else, of any he can meet with that are not friends or allies of his Majesty." The profit from the plunder of the *Seahorse* was estimated at the equivalent of $5 million U.S. dollars.

One of the earliest individual privateers to achieve fame was Francis Drake. In 1580, Queen Elizabeth I knighted him on the deck of the *Golden Hind,* calling him her "dear Pyrat." Drake's three-year voyage around the world attacking Spanish colonies paid dividends to his backers (suspected to include Elizabeth) at the rate of forty-seven to one. As is no doubt becoming clear to the reader, privateering, like funds management in the twentieth century, became an industry.

Elizabeth tried to regulate privateering during the seventeenth century by establishing "prize courts," through which seized

Privateer Treasure Seekers

In England, the earliest "letters of marque" or reprisal commissions were issued in the thirteenth century, such as King John's commission to Eustace the Monk around A.D. 1200 to plunder French vessels in the Channel. In 1212 the perfidious Monk accepted the better terms of King Phillip of France, and was killed during an attempted invasion of England.

Edward I (1272–1307) granted "commissions of reprisal to owners of merchant ships that had been plundered illegally at sea." Many of these merchant vessels combined trade with plunder of other shipping, so that the boundaries between legitimate trade, reprisal, and outright piracy became blurred.

The gentry of the English south coast, Welsh seaboard, and east coast of Ireland invested in privateering/piracy in the sixteenth century and protected their employees against rare intrusions of the law. The seventeenth century saw the age of the organized investor, epitomized in England by the East India Company, which in 1600 obtained a royal charter for sole access to the "whole, entire and only trade and traffic to the East Indies." The early voyages of the Company were similar to other ventures at the time in that they were for the sake of quick gains from daring enterprise. Only later, with domination of the India trade, did the Company adopt its powerful conservative role in the English establishment.

The Dutch were equally powerful on the seas. In 1621 the West India Company was formed with the aim of "humbling the pride and might of Spain." Following a victory in 1628 over a Spanish treasure fleet, the Dutch West India Company declared a 50% dividend. This coup had the wider reverberation of damaging Spanish credit in Europe, and financing a vigorous trade offensive by the Dutch in Brazil. An older organization, the Dutch East India Company, at its height in 1669 owned 150 merchant ships and 40 warships, and could put 10,000 soldiers in the field.

Box 1-3.

prize goods were sold and the proceeds distributed according to the commission agreement. A common distribution was investors, 40–50%; the Crown, 10%; Admiralty, 6%; captain, 3–5%; officers total, 6–10%; crew total, 15–20%.

Privateering was in the eye of the beholder. In 1634, the East India Company complained bitterly about the behavior of privateers with a commission from Charles I, as that of "the king's pirates," though its own privateers had operated similarly. Of course the company was probably of similar opinion to Sir Walter Raleigh, who is reputed to have observed, "Did you ever know of any that were pirates for millions? They that only work for small things, are pirates."

The seventeenth and eighteenth centuries were the golden ages of piracy, when euphemisms abounded to hide the true nature of the naval merchant venturer. "Going on the account" was a popular term in the English colonies which became the United States of America. "Roving" and "being at the seas" were other terms.

On the Spanish Main (mainland of Spanish America, the Caribbean, and West Indies) the common term was *buccaneer.* Buccaneers were originally hunters who cooked and dried their meat over a green wood lattice called "bucan" by Carib natives. The French *boucanier* became *buccaneer* when these hunters turned to the sea, initially attacking shipping close to land.

The French did not refer to the Caribbean pirates as "buccaneers," but rather as *flibustiers,* which was a corrupt translation of another English euphemism, "freebooters." The term remains in use today, corrupted once again to *filibuster,* to describe the actions of orators who plunder time to delay legislation in parliament or congress.

In the Mediterranean, *corsair* was the term used to describe those who cruised (from *corsaire,* "to cruise") the ocean looking to plunder, sometimes under commission as privateers, and at other times simply as pirates of the Barbary Coast. Christopher Columbus sailed as a Corsican corsair under the French flag in 1485, before his famous voyage opened up the Americas to European speculation.

Continual outbreaks of war meant that pirates were commissioned in wartime to act as auxiliaries to inadequate navies. Commissions also came to be traded, initially transferred with the ship, from owner to owner. Officials in Caribbean and American

Captain Kidd

The legendary New York pirate Captain William Kidd was granted a commission by King William in 1695 "to make purchase of French shipping." He was hanged as a pirate in 1701 at least in part for plundering an Indian ship sailing under French passes which could not be produced for his trial. The passes were found over a hundred years later, part of evidence which suggests that Kidd's trial was political and under the influence of the East India Company. Kidd was in fact an inept privateer rather than a pirate, but in the eyes of the public throughout the years he simply became the source of legendary buried pirate treasure.

Since he resided on Wall Street, in New York, years before trading began on the New York Stock Exchange, it might be said that Captain Kidd was the first Wall Street pirate.

Box 1-4.

colonies could issue commissions, and "letters of marque" were bought and sold, issued in blank, forged, altered, and redated, so that, even under regulation, the line between piracy and privateering became blurred.

Sir Francis Drake was a hero to the English and a pirate to the Spaniards. William Kidd was a privateer, though he was hanged as a pirate. John Paul was the seafaring son of a gardener on Lord Selkirk's estate near Kircumbright in Scotland. With his name changed to John Paul Jones, he became one of the most daring privateers of the War of Independence and a hero to Americans. When he raided the coasts of England, Scotland, and Ireland, Englishmen denounced him as a pirate.

The fund manager George Soros no doubt considers himself an astute manager of funds on commission, but in 1992, after a highly publicized attack on the pound sterling, the English public denounced him as a speculative pirate.

The evolution of naval warfare and the growth of regular navies allowed governments to curb piracy between wars. In the mid-seventeenth century, pirates found American colonies more advantageous than the Caribbean as land bases, not least because of the welcome afforded by American merchants, disaffected with the English attempts at trade monopoly. Pirates became privateers in the War of Independence.

Although politicians marked a difference between privateering and piracy, there was little distinction in the minds of naval officers. Naval morale was encouraged by the sharing of the proceeds from captured prize ships, and of course privateers reduced the opportunities for prizes. The great English admiral Lord Nelson expressed this dislike for competition in more political terms when he said, in 1804, "The conduct of all privateers is, as far as I have seen, so near piracy that I can only wonder any civilized nation can allow them."

Jean Lafitte's pirates defended the city of New Orleans in the War of 1812, thus qualifying as privateers and becoming heroes. After Great Britain was forced to the negotiating table, Lafitte and his men resumed their piracy cum smuggling operation. Lafitte

Privateers of the War of 1812

The British navy certainly had a reason to dislike privateers during the War of 1812, which produced the first sign of U.S. technological superiority. Specially built, superbly fast sailing vessels outclassed the standard British naval ships. New York alone fitted out 120 cruisers, which brought in 275 prizes and destroyed many more. One crew came back with $300,000 worth of plunder after dodging 17 pursuers. The *True Blooded Yankee* accounted for 27 vessels in 37 days, and her crew realized $3 million in prize money, including substantial government bounties. Profits were so assured that the New York legislature passed an Act to Encourage Privateering Associations.

By 1815 the British navy could demonstrate maritime superiority without the need for privateers. The move by the great nations to outlaw privateering as well as pirates commenced with the establishment of regular navies, but did not come to fruition until the Treaty of Paris in 1856.

Box 1-5.

was reported killed in 1823, but some say he escaped to end his days peacefully in Paris. Legend has it that the old pirate and privateer helped to finance another rebel, a scholar named Karl Marx, who later inspired attacks on capitalist wealth.

The United States did not ratify the 1856 Treaty of Paris, on the basis that it could not afford a regular navy (see Box 1-5). Privateers thus operated during the American Civil War, especially for the Confederacy. The last privateer is thought to have been the Confederate submarine *Hunley,* which became the world's first submarine to sink a warship, the blockade ship *Housatonic,* outside Charleston in February 1864. Unfortunately the crew of the *Hunley* did not live to enjoy their triumph. The *Hunley* vanished after the attack; its hull was rediscovered in 1995.

The Nineteenth Century—Privateering Dies; Speculation Lives

The demise of privateers and piracy coincided with the successful introduction of paper money by England in the period 1797 to 1823. Throughout the nineteenth century and the advance of the Industrial Revolution, the circulation of gold and silver coins ceased in most countries in favor of paper money. It is probably only coincidence that the increase in use of paper money occurred at the same time as opportunities in stock market speculation from companies' share fluctuations grew in the early period of capitalism.

Andrew Dickson White wrote of the 1790s in *Fiat Money Inflation in France:* "Out of the inflation of prices grew a speculating class. In the complete uncertainty as to the future, all business became a game of chance and all businessmen gamblers. . . . Instead of satisfaction with legitimate profits, came a passion for inordinate gains." The speculation which occurred in France in the 1790s and in the United Kingdom in 1815 was followed by booms and busts in 1819 (United States), 1825 (United Kingdom), and 1837 (United States), which set a speculative pattern in stock markets through to the present day.

Nathan Rothschild—Extraordinary Speculator

In 1815 the English demonstrated that speculative excess was a natural by-product of industrial capitalism. The speculation that in past wars was a motive for privateering manifested itself in the Napoleonic wars in the paper financial markets of stocks and bonds. The actions of Nathan Rothschild around the time of the 1815 Battle of Waterloo demonstrated that the well-financed stock trader with sound strategy and intelligence could make bigger profits than a seagoing privateer.

In the days before the decisive battle, many investors sold shares in case the Duke of Wellington lost, and British commercial interests were damaged. One who took the contrarian view was Nathan Rothschild, head of the Rothschild banking house in London, and agent of the British government in supplying subsidies to the powers opposing Napoleon. The Rothschild buying was known by many but discounted to some degree because of Rothschild's close relationship with the government.

Rothschild's information service was second to none, and he was in fact the first to know the results of the Battle of Waterloo, by carrier pigeon. Realizing that the public knew of his previous stock buying and the reputation of his intelligence service, Rothschild commenced selling on the London stock market. The crowd assumed that Napoleon had won, and sold shares in panic. The stock market collapsed.

Once the market reached bargain levels, Rothschild bought, only hours before Wellington's victory at Waterloo became public knowledge. A wave of buying by the relieved crowd then pushed shares to near boom prices. Rothschild was reputed to have made the then fortune of £1 million in a single day.

His public relations must have also been superior because, far from being accused of manipulation, he was reputed to have saved the stock market from collapse by buying shares from frightened investors in the darkest hour.

Box 1-6.

Futures markets were established in Japan around 1730 as a risk protection mechanism for the all-important rice market. In 1869, trading became so speculative and chaotic that risk protection was not possible. The market was closed for two years, then reopened with new rules.

The Chicago Board of Trade was established in 1851 to provide price risk protection to grain traders. Unfortunately it did not take long before U.S. commodity exchanges were considered gambling dens. In 1867, the Illinois Legislature passed a law which provided that the parties to futures contracts (referred to in the law as gambling contracts) should be fined and imprisoned. The law was repealed the following year, but was indicative of the speculative fever which was seen again in the following century in the 1920s, 1980s, and 1990s.

I am not claiming here that the demise of the seagoing commissioned privateer gave rise to the financial speculator, although it is an idea that psychologists and economists might ponder. What I will state is that financial speculation today has at least as much, if not more, influence on the global economy as did piracy in the seventeenth century. *Managed Account Reports* suggests that the amount of money in commodity and hedge funds exceeds $175 billion, which when leveraged could apply nearly $2 trillion in market power. In addition it was estimated in 1995 that the top 10 commercial banks in the world had trading accounts of $140 billion.

Alternatively revered and reviled, large hedge fund managers such as Paul Tudor Jones and Stanley Druckenmiller move millions of dollars around the globe in a relentless search for speculative profits. In financial circles, the actions of managers such as these are discussed with the same awe as men of early days discussed the actions of the buccaneer Sir Henry Morgan.

My research indicates that the principles applied by successful privateers in their careers can be applied to speculative operations in twentieth-century financial markets. Pirates were not always the romantic figures in search of buried treasure popularized in books such as Robert Louis Stevenson's *Treasure Island.* They were entrepreneurs, serious in their pursuit of riches, at the risk of their lives, in an ill-educated era which valued lives cheaply. Pirates of yesteryear were nothing like today's illegal peddlers of intellectual property whom the media has branded modern "pirates."

Privateering has been an honorable, if dangerous, profession since the age of classical Greece. A well-provisioned privateer, captained by a daring man with a mission and good intelligence, could capture immense riches, at limited risk. It is my opinion that some privateers can be used as role models by today's serious speculators who wish to attack the markets with a mission of consistent profits and controlled risk.

Speculation in modern markets can be an extremely profitable financial adventure for the average trader, but to achieve success one must chart a course with at least as much care as any ancient mariner seeking prizes in dangerous waters. I believe that the privateer allegory can assist the speculator in financial markets to approach the twenty-first century with confidence. By adapting age-old privateer policy and strategic mindset to modern tactical resources of computer technology, the reader should be able to formulate his or her own trading plan to achieve consistent leveraged profits.

If you want success, you must develop an attitude that will achieve success. Throughout this book I shall offer techniques formulated from thirty years of market experience, in a privateer mindset that the reader can use to formulate his or her own planned attitude for success.

With my guidance, you will need to determine your own policy or privateer commission mindset. I shall offer computer-assisted strategies to those who can spend only limited time analyzing the markets. These strategies have had proven success in financial markets since at least 1992. I shall indicate the technical analysis indicators which will give today's professional market privateer the edge in implementing strategies or even just trading successfully in the near term.

2 Policy for Speculation: Privateer's Commission

What Is Speculation?

When I joined a Japanese trading company after my term in the Royal Australian Navy, part of my responsibility came to be the weekly tabulation of the wool portfolio. My division traded greasy wool, which in this raw form has thousands of types, all involving different variants of wool fiber quality and fineness. The company sold wool forward—that is, it contracted to deliver a specific type of raw wool to an overseas mill, at a contracted price, at a future time. It held stocks of wool, and it traded the wool futures market.

The Australian wool division operated independently from the company head office in Japan, but the balance of our portfolio could not exceed a particular limit. The balance of the portfolio consisted of our forward commitment to overseas mills of various wools; our wool stocks, often of different types of wools; and the futures market position of bought or sold contracts. It was my job to value all these elements in order to calculate the balance of the wool portfolio in U.S. dollar terms.

The Japanese general manager of the wool division had the power to increase the forward commitments, or purchase new wool stocks and order trades carried out on the Sydney Greasy Wool Futures Exchange. At the end of the week, as his assistant, I had the power to say whether or not the balance of our portfolio was within the limits set by the head office in Japan. It was the result of my calculations which were communicated to the head office. The importance of this role might explain why my boss took a great deal of time to explain his opinions of future market movements to a rather minor subordinate.

My Japanese mentor was unusual for a senior manager in that organization in that he was willing to take sole responsibility for his decisions without relying on the normal cultural consensus. If he thought the price of wool would rise, he would encourage other managers to increase stocks and/or bought futures contracts so that our portfolio balance was heavily in the black. We often made money faster in a falling market because of large forward commitments outweighing small stocks, in addition to sold futures contracts. My concurrence with the general manager's forecast of price movement meant that my subjective valuation of individual wool types allowed us always to be within the limit set by our head office.

Although we were designated as a Japanese merchant trading house, we knew that we were speculating in wool. We knew that, at times, when we were slightly in excess of our trading limit, we held a speculative position which could present a financial loss if we were wrong. It was due to the skill of the manager, with some small assistance from me, that our speculative positions in general were very successful, so that the company became the world's largest wool buyer. We were always prepared to contain losses if necessary.

Influenced as I am by my past experience, I define speculation as *the purchase or sale of objects with the calculated intention of resale or repurchase at a later time at a more profitable price.*

Trading of commodities is speculation. Trading of commodities futures contracts is leveraged speculation. Buying of real estate, without regard to rental income or home use, is speculation. The purchase of stocks on the stock exchange, for capital gain without regard to dividend income, is speculation. Trading of stock and money derivatives is leveraged speculation.

In addition to my own experience, my definition owes much to Benjamin Graham, a respected American investor and teacher who in his 1934 textbook *Security Analysis* stated: "An investment operation is one, which upon thorough analysis promises safety of principal and an adequate return. Operations not meeting these requirements are speculative."

I am aware that my definition, or that of Graham, might not be widely accepted in the 1990s, particularly by treasurers and fund managers. My narrow view of investment means that most activities undertaken in the stock market, real estate market, bond market, and foreign exchange market are speculative. This would mean that many public funds, supposedly conservatively invested, could be defined as speculative.

Financial institutions in particular are today as fond of euphemism as were eighteenth-century pirates. Treasuries of banks and large corporations do not speculate—they "position take," "over hedge," and "cover risk with leveraged derivatives." Many people in Orange County, California, have now discovered that holding leveraged derivatives equates to speculation.

My definition of speculation will not alter the outlook of those committed to the trading culture of the late 1980s and early 1990s. This is not my purpose. My definition is proposed so that the reader of this book is in no doubt that the acceptance of financial risk for the purpose of gain is speculation. *Once speculation is admitted, the risk can be managed,* in particular with the strategies that I demonstrate in later chapters.

A nineteenth-century president of the New York Cotton Exchange, Dickson G. Watts, defined *speculation* as a "venture with calculation," and *gambling* as a "venture without calculation."

At an early age, I was informed by my father that betting on the horse races was "a sucker's game" and that only the "bookies" won. However, at a later age I devised a system for betting on the horses which was successful over a long period, even though the return would have been less than bank interest. Long after I had ceased betting on the horses, I met a professional "punter" who carried out an incredible amount of research into his own handicapping and who operated to a plan. He would place a bet at the racetrack to win his planned amount. If that bet succeeded, he would leave the track. If the initial bet failed, he would need to win back that bet plus his planned amount, and would place the second bet accordingly. If the second bet failed, the successive bets would need to be increased until he won his planned amount. That man was never a multimillionaire, but lived a very comfortable lifestyle and could be considered successful. The punter's secrets were:

- That he researched the races on which he bet
- That he was sufficiently capitalized
- That he operated to a plan

Under Dickson Watts' definition, my professional punter friend was not a gambler but a speculator. Casinos make similar judgments against "card counters" playing blackjack. People caught using a calculated method to beat house odds will be asked to leave the blackjack tables and often the casino itself, because they are not considered gamblers.

When traders play the markets, only they, and their banker, know whether they are gamblers or speculators.

Policy Formulation

Once speculation is admitted, the corporation or individual speculator can form guidelines to limit any financial or emotional damage which might occur if the speculative venture goes wrong.

As I explained in Chapter 1, the main difference between a privateer and a pirate was that the privateer carried a commission from a government authorizing the taking of prizes. It is true that many of these commissions were tainted, particularly those sold by the early governors of the American colonies. Nevertheless the existence of a commission saved a number of men from the gallows. Adherence to a well-planned commission was responsible for many rich rewards to a number of disciplined privateers.

The modern-day market privateer cannot obtain a "commission to speculate" from a king. Today's governments do not issue commissions, even though they do sanction speculation and often benefit from higher rates of taxation on that activity. The modern-day individual privateer must create a personal commission by forming a policy which he or she is prepared to follow in a speculative plan.

A corporate speculative policy will be formed when the board and management fully consider the risks they are willing to assume in the company's financial activities in reaching for corporate goals, and the capability of the company to manage those risks.

In this book I shall address most of my comments to the individual speculator, but my recommendations can in general be adopted by any corporation willing to admit to speculation.

The speculator, with his or her partner, must outline a plan or policy that he or she is willing to follow in speculative activity during the course of the next 3 to 5 years. Examination of the following factors is suggested:

- Financial goals
- Financial and personal resources
- Acceptable risk
- Manageable strategies

After examination of these factors by all decision makers in the partnership, the policy should be written down, preferably on a single sheet of paper, and kept in view in the work area. It is not necessary for the policy to be written or displayed, but this encourages discipline, which is the main element of successful speculation, particularly if the partners are married.

Financial Goals

Lewis Carroll's character in *Alice in Wonderland* said, "Would you tell me please, which way I ought to go from here?" The Cheshire Cat replied: "That depends a good deal on where you want to get to."

Where do you want to get to? What are your goals?

The reason for undertaking speculation is generally to achieve financial advancement at a faster pace than might occur through labor or investment. One should undertake acceptance of risks only if the goals are finite and attainable. Maybe a list of goals can

Goals

Goals should be:

Tangible	Results should be able to be measured
Suitable	Should be appropriate for the particular speculator
Valuable	Value above cost can be financial or social
Achievable	Should not be too ambitious within the time frame
Flexible	On the margins, while main aim is observed
Within time frame	Deadline needs to be defined
Committed	Unanimous approval has to be achieved

Box 2-1.

be made, and reduced to two or three of the most important and achievable.

If a speculator's only goal is excitement, this also should be recognized. The majority of speculators that I have encountered over the years traded for excitement, but would never admit this to themselves. Excitement can be a legitimate goal, but if trading is also to be profitable, then maybe exciting trading should only occur spasmodically when the time is absolutely right. Disciplined trading still has elements of excitement, but admittedly can become boring when a position reaches a riskless profit level.

Financial and Personal Resources

The individual speculator must decide how much capital to risk. Even though good trading strategies can reduce risk, one cannot escape the fact that the speculation with the most rewards tends to be high risk. It is my belief that the speculator needs to be psychologically prepared to lose all the risk capital.

When one trades with capital that might be needed for other purposes, there is a psychological tendency to ignore trading strategy in preference to defense of capital; tactics can be made defensive, which negates the whole idea of speculative attack.

Although speculative capital, apart from futures margins, does not need to be wholly in cash, it does have to be in a liquid form of asset. I suggest that the amount of capital be specified in the policy, or even that a specific account be established separate from investment accounts. Any alteration to the amount of available speculative capital should call for a total reappraisal of policy by all partners.

The capital available for futures trading should be more than is required to cover the initial margin. As a general rule of thumb, I have often suggested that 3 times the amount of initial margin is needed to trade a leveraged market. On the S&P 500 futures market, the deposit might be as high as $35,000, which means that on the conservative side capital of $105,000 per contract needs to be set aside to trade. This level of risk is not acceptable to many speculators.

It is possible that the speculative strategy will not call for positions to be held overnight or that the win/loss ratio of the strategy is such that a capital of 3 times the deposit might seem excessive. If this is the case, the capital ratio can be reduced later when the operation of the strategy proves successful.

The novice speculator will need to spend some of the capital on education, in proving the trading strategy, so it is important that a tolerant financial cushion exists. It is no use spending money, through losses, on learning, only to have insufficient capital to profit from those hard knock lessons.

In addition to capital, the speculator needs to commit personal resources, knowledge, time, and temperament.

The most important factor in speculation is the temperament of the speculator. As already mentioned, it is my observation that the majority of speculators trade because of the excitement of participating in markets in which large amounts of money can be won and lost quickly. The psychological boost is similar to the one from visiting the racetrack or casino. The casual speculator and gambler may know that the odds favor the professionals—the bookmakers or "the house"—but that is secondary to the rush of excitement caused by small wins and the potential to win big.

Losses at the end of the day are passed off as the cost of the excitement of play.

Readers who like to speculate casually in the manner of gambling need read no further, because my advice is more likely to curb their pleasure than make them money. Successful speculation is undertaken at the expense of curbing the emotions, forgoing much of the reward of excitement in favor of financial return.

The act of curbing one's emotions can be termed self-discipline, which is probably the most important facet of a successful speculator's character. I have also found that self-esteem is an integral part of self-discipline.

As in life, the person most likely to succeed in speculation is one who has developed the confidence in her or his ability to learn and adapt to changing circumstances. The excitement of trading futures and stock markets is due to their constant state of flux. Constant change means that those participating will eventually make mistakes.

Speculators who have self-esteem will treat each mistake as a learning experience, something to examine to see whether changes are necessary to the trading plan or whether the mistake simply occurred due to a market aberration. These traders do not blame the markets for their losses. Because they have confidence in their own ability, they allow the markets to tell them how to trade. This self-confidence allows them to make decisions, not necessarily with the crowd, and exercise the self-discipline to follow those decisions.

Those without confidence in their own ability tend to need others' opinions and therefore someone to blame for mistakes. If one does not accept responsibility for mistakes, there is little need for self-discipline. The fault can always be made to rest with someone else's lack of discipline.

Self-discipline and self-esteem cannot be learned from books. Character needs to be formed from firsthand experience, but the learning curve can be shortened by using others' experiences as a guide. There are a number of books available which examine the psychology of the speculator. Among those that I have found helpful are Jake Berstein's *Investor Quotient* and *Beyond Investor Quotient* and Mark Douglas' *The Disciplined Trader.*

Keeping to a trading strategy is one way of ensuring a disciplined approach to speculation, but it requires self-discipline not to deviate from the plan without just cause.

Fear and Greed

The main emotions which move markets are fear and greed. The successful speculator not only needs to be able to curb those emotions within himself or herself, but to recognize these emotions as motivating factors of others in market movements.

Rudyard Kipling wrote of keeping one's head when all about were losing theirs. Such disciplined actions are imperative in speculation. Running with the crowd is a natural human trait. At times this behavior can produce success in the markets, but at key times the successful speculator will leave the market to the crowds because participation is no longer logical.

Observe the actions of people crossing roads at traffic lights. There is no doubting the existence of national or regional behavior. New York pedestrians, who tend to flout authority, often take no notice of traffic signals and abuse those who nearly collide with them. In Tokyo, pedestrians are likely to wait patiently until the traffic light turns green and cross the road as a crowd with few leaders or stragglers. In London, one can observe those independent souls who anticipate the changing traffic light, the majority who obey the traffic signals, and those stragglers who are nearly run over after the light has signaled danger.

In financial markets, the most profitable trades are those which have anticipated the entry of the crowd, and which are quit before the crowd finds reason to leave. This means that the speculator must conquer the fear of acting independently from the crowd, possibly with a trading system which can choose an early, but not too early, entry point. Like the stepping out of the "too early" pedestrian against the traffic signal, too early an entry into the market can mean a crushing loss.

Once in the market, the speculator must conquer the greed that sustains the crowd that is staying in the market and increasing positions because of potential profits. The speculator must choose an exit point well before the crowd starts to feel uncomfortable and be driven by fear of losses to quit the market. The legendary U.S. investor of the 1930s, Bernard Baruch, when asked the secret of his success in the stock markets, stated that he always sold too early. He always quit ahead of the crowd.

On the odd occasion, an event will occur which will panic the crowd, such as the 1987 stock market crash or 1994 bond collapse. The more successful speculator in all likelihood will have quit before any panic, because of system signals or other signs (my technical system was short prior to both falls). However, the speculator needs to be able to take actions independently of panic-induced fear. Money management stop-loss orders are a part of a trading plan which should be triggered quickly. Thus the speculator is basically following the rule that *controlled* panic can represent survival, as long as action is undertaken early. Stop-losses once entered should not be altered without good reason,

Discipline

On August 1, 1708, the privateer Woodes Rogers sailed from Bristol with the commission to pursue, attack, and seize enemy ships in the South Sea. The enemy was France allied to Spain.

The first ship sighted in the Atlantic was pursued and forced to heave to, but Rogers then found that the vessel was a neutral Swedish merchant outside his commission. He allowed the ship to proceed without any confiscation of cargo.

Because their pay depended on rich prizes, Rogers' men protested in a mutinous outburst. Rogers immediately clapped 10 seamen in irons and had the ringleader lashed with a knotted rope. He explained to the remainder of the crew why the Swedish ship was outside the privateering commission.

This display of discipline was to prove important later in Rogers' three-year voyage around the world. Of course Rogers was maybe lucky that, soon after the Swedish incident, his larcenous crew was satisfied by the capture of a small Spanish barque. Nevertheless, the need for discipline had been demonstrated.

Box 2-2.

because this often leads to later panic-induced heavy losses. It is far better to quit early in a crisis, and possibly to reenter later when the crowd has settled down to tend its wounds.

Tony Plummer of Hambros Bank has written an intriguing book, *Forecasting Financial Markets,* which can be recommended as lucidly explaining the actions of the crowd and the importance of crowd psychology in the market. He also discusses technical analysis, which to my mind is the tool which best affords confidence to take decisions independently from the crowd.

Time Frame

Another key factor which the speculator must discover in his or her character is the time frame which is most comfortable. Stock market investors who have experience at holding stocks for long periods of time are often uncomfortable trading in volatile markets which might call for trading positions intraday. Bank treasurers who have experience at trading volatile money markets intraday often experience discomfort at holding leveraged positions overnight, let alone for some weeks.

It has been my experience that speculators are swayed by events and news which affect their particular time frame. The casual speculator relies often on news reports which either report an event after its action on the market or forecast likely happenings which will affect the market in coming days or weeks. The foreign exchange dealer or bond futures speculator, who views a computer screen constantly, tends to be influenced by intraday movements. The danger to the speculator is that the time frame of *influence* can be mistaken for the time frame of *action.*

Losses have been common for speculators acting on newspaper reports the day following an event, when the market had already begun discounting that event's influence. Losses have also occurred from speculators acting today, anticipating events not due for some weeks.

Nor are professional traders exempt from this mix of time frames. For many years I have criticized the hedge advice from bank foreign exchange dealers because it is often given, based on near-term influences, to hedgers whose time frame is 3 months or more in the future. Professional bond dealers have been known to take a position based on an outlook of days or weeks, and then quit, following an intraday panic, only to reenter some ticks worse off because the longer-term opinion was unchanged.

It is not possible to recommend a particular time frame for all speculators. Personally I am uncomfortable trading off screens or jobbing on the floor on intraday moves. I prefer taking a position for days or weeks. In any speculative position that I might take, I follow a technical system, but do allow fundamental events due in following days to have some influence. In terms of technical analysis, I focus on the daily, weekly, and monthly time frames to feel comfortable and then take action within the daily time frame. I have found that most technical analysts tend to be position takers like I am, with a longer-term time frame than many fundamental traders.

I know a number of successful speculators who take only intra-

Time Frame Focus

Speculation in the Japanese yen has been popular in the 1990s, but losses have occurred because many speculators lost focus on their time frame.

The legendary swordsman Miyamoto Musashi, in his famous seventeenth-century book, *The Book of Five Rings,* gives advice for martial arts that can be used in speculation:

> The eyes are to be focused in such a way as to maximize the range and breadth of vision. Observation and perception are two separate things; the observing eye is stronger, the perceiving eye is weaker. A speciality of martial arts is to see that which is far away closely, and to see that which is nearby from a distance.

The speculative trader needs to focus on the near-term time frame, but be extremely aware of the fit of the near term into long-term time frame analysis.

Box 2-3.

day positions, either by jobbing on the floor or using computer screens in financial institution offices. The majority of these traders use a mix of technical analysis and "gut feel." One professional uses only the gut feel of a natural trader and enjoys the lack of stress from not holding positions overnight. Another trader uses modern technology in the form of tick-by-tick graphs in a system developed by the Chicago Board of Trade called *Market Profile,* and profitably varies his trading between 1 hour and 2 days.

The successful speculator will be aware of the time frame in which he or she is most comfortable and arrange the strategy accordingly. The unplanned mixture of time frames should be avoided. One successful short-term jobber of my experience went so far as to ignore the daily and weekly fundamentals, because they could interfere with his analysis of intraday market movements.

In summary, I would suggest that the speculator be aware of both long- and short-term trends, but focus only on one time frame to trade.

Bull or Bear?

I would also suggest that the speculator examine his or her nature to discover whether he or she has the tendency to seek rising or falling markets. In my experience most speculators are natural bulls, possibly because of past stock market activity. My own tendency is to look toward bear markets, possibly due to my early history with a firm that benefited, often heavily, from falling prices.

There is no particular advantage to being a natural bear or a natural bull. I simply recommend that the tendency to seek one market or the other be recognized, so that any entry or exit is based on a true signal and not on one that might be tainted by the natural desire for a rise or fall.

In summary, in forming your speculative policy you must "know yourself." As George Goodman, under his nom de plume "Adam Smith," said in his book *The Money Game:* "If you don't know who you are, this is an expensive place to find out."

Acceptable Risk

The individual speculator must decide at the outset the level of tolerance to risk on individual trades. The overall risk will be established by the amount of capital, but the premise of speculation is that losses will occur because of the risky nature of the venture. Any individual losses should not be large enough to damage the total capital, so as to prevent further speculation to recoup losses.

The level of risk will first depend on the temperament of the speculator, which I have discussed. The two other major factors are the markets in which one is to speculate and a money management plan.

It is not within the scope of this book to examine markets in detail. Any Exchange in the world can suggest books which will describe and give advice on trading its markets.

Many speculators confine themselves to one market which they know well, such as the U.S. stock market. They trade only the stocks that they know well, utilizing different trading strategies according to the prevailing sentiment on those stocks. The acceptable level of risk is well within their comfort zone.

On the other hand, like many ancient privateers, my prizes come from the international universe, because the strategy that I will outline allows acceptable risk in many markets. Diversified risk means that many markets need to be studied before a few are chosen for high rewards.

While the structure of a market is easily checked, the nature of each market and its idiosyncrasies can be discovered only from a broker or a specialist in that market. A market is made up of its participants: Who is willing to buy? Who is willing to sell? What motivates their actions? Some markets are heavily influenced by locals—floor traders—whereas others are dominated by large hedgers.

Bond futures markets, for instance, tend to be influenced by institutional speculators who trade in large blocks in a very short time frame using fairly timid technical analysis. Asian stock index futures have lost a large number of these small-tick institutional speculators, except maybe in Japan, but have gained institutional arbitrage players with longer time frames and higher tolerance to market price movement.

Identification of market movers and shakers is important when formulating a trading strategy. I have found from experience that markets with a large short-time-frame, speculative element respond well to volatility-based systems. Markets heavily influenced by hedgers or longer-time-frame speculators show good results from trend-following systems.

In addition to market participants, one must be aware of the relative influence of outside markets and the period of that influence. A large number of international stock markets and stock index futures are influenced by actions in the U.S. markets, yet at other times individual markets can ignore or exacerbate the movements of the Dow Jones Industrial Average Index. In 1994, the U.S. stock market had a correction, but the London share market and LIFFE Share Price Index futures market turned this correction into a major fall, as illustrated in Graph 2-1. My analysis at that time was that a number of portfolio managers took profits from the U.K. market and invested in the U.S. market, which was seen, correctly at the time, as having more potential.

Interest rate, bond, and currency markets are subject to varying amounts of government intervention at different times. A government floor or ceiling can mean that changes might be necessary to mechanical or computerized systems. At other times, intervention can simply indicate that the markets are best left alone unless one wishes to speculate in the direction that the government is nudging the market.

Commodities futures markets were once regarded as markets with extreme risk. In the 1990s, when even conservative municipal funds play the financial derivatives markets, I have found that commodities futures often behave more rationally than the so-called low-risk government bond markets.

If one uses a good technical strategy, one does not need to be an expert in the commodities he or she trades. It is normally enough to know the motivations of the larger price movers, the effects of weather and of labor and shipping problems, and the seasonal price behavior of each commodity.

Some commodities are downright perverse. The silver futures market is a good example of schizoid market behavior. Silver can be rising strongly under the influence of the precious metals, gold

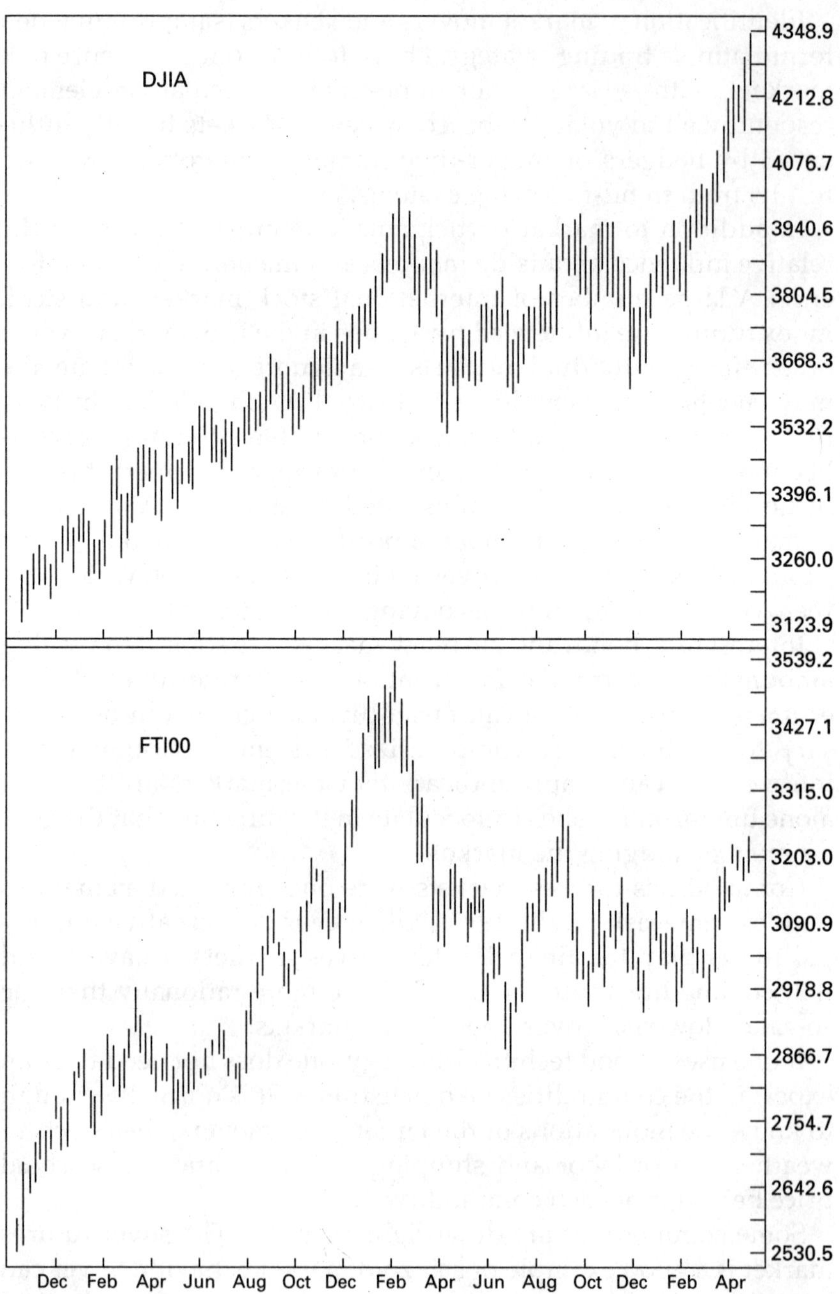

Graph 2-1. Relationship of New York Dow Jones Industrial Average to London FT 100.

and platinum, then just as suddenly fall because base metals fall, even though gold might continue to rise. When one knows the market, it can often be discerned that the rise was speculative until the level was reached where hedging became attractive to base-metal miners to whom silver is a by-product. Thus the influence of other precious metals markets can be illusory over the longer term but speculatively satisfactory in the short term.

Leverage

The size of each speculative bet will depend on the nature of each market, and on the minimum entry level. Many stock and bond markets do not allow leverage, so the full value of stocks or bonds needs to be paid. There is comfort to many speculators in knowing that they cannot lose more than they have laid out. This is the reason that option markets are popular—any loss is predetermined, but any profits can be as high as the sky.

Futures markets and some stock markets allow operations on margin, which allows speculation to be highly leveraged. The capital required to speculate in these markets is directly related to the initial margin required on individual markets. Clearinghouses of futures exchanges establish the initial margin, generally based on overnight volatility. They try not to change the size of the initial margin frequently to avoid further disturbance to the markets.

In some countries, such as Japan, the government agency responsible for the regulation of markets can influence the size of the initial margin. The initial margins on the Osaka Nikkei Index and New York S&P 500 futures contracts often appear to be high (post the 1987 crash) relative to daily volatility, due to government influence.

One of the reasons for high volume and high volatility in many high-initial-margin markets such as the S&P 500 is that traders overcome the barrier of high initial margin by day trading. Institutions and high-net-worth individuals can use their credit ratings and collateral to buy and sell large positions in the course of one day without the need to deposit the full cash value of initial margins, because positions are not held overnight.

It is doubtful that a novice speculator will trade successfully on a day-trading or jobbing strategy. I will give some hints in a later chapter on day trading because the widespread use of computers has made "jobbing" extremely popular. In my opinion, markets such as the S&P 500 which can have *intraday* volatility 3 times the average *interday* volatility, are for experienced market pirates with well-formed tactical skills. I prefer the less exciting privateer strategy of enjoying highly profitable long trend runs.

Stops

The degree of risk acceptable can be managed through use of various techniques in any market. A strategy should provide the reasons for logically entering and getting out of any position, whether or not it eventually proves profitable. Once a position is taken in the market, a price level can do nothing but rise, fall, or move sideways.

Although the trader must have provisions in the strategy that govern when to take profits and how long to remain in an inactive market, the key to money management is the provision for limiting loss at times when a position shows adversity. The most common and certainly the most valid method of exiting from a losing trade is the stop-loss order.

A *stop-loss order,* often simply called a "stop," is an order to buy or sell at market price when the market reaches a designated price. A stop-loss order to buy must be entered above the prevailing market price. A stop-loss order to sell must be entered below the prevailing market price. Many disciplined traders place their stop-loss orders immediately as their original position is initiated. That way, when their planned potential loss is reached, they are not tempted to add to their loss by diverging from the plan in giving the market a few points more to reverse direction.

Depending on a speculator's knowledge and skill, other money management techniques can be included in trading strategy to make levels of risk acceptable. I will include some of my methods later in this book. Further study, including reading of books such as those by Ralph Vince (*Portfolio Management Formulas, Mathematics of Money Management*) and Nauzer Balsara (*Money Management Strategies for Futures Traders*), is recommended.

Manageable Strategies

The purpose of a defined speculative policy is to have guidelines established which the speculator intends to follow for the time frame of the speculative program.

The ancient Chinese general Sun Tsu wrote in *The Art of War:* "War is a matter of vital importance to the State. It concerns the lives and deaths of the people; and affects the survival or demise of the State. It must be thoroughly studied." Speculation can be as damaging to the health of the individual as war can be to the state. It requires commitment. Politicians promise. Conquerors commit.

Policy establishes how the speculative war is to be fought—the rules of warfare. Actual battle strategies need to be examined and approved before war is waged. The strategy need not be in detailed form in the policy, but the general type should be recognized.

In essence a trading plan is simple—it has to indicate when to enter the market and when to quit. In practice the ultimate decision to buy or sell can be influenced by a complex amalgam of factors.

First, the speculator has to decide whether to follow a mechanical system or one based on continuing assessment of risk/reward. In my opinion this choice will rest on the amount of self-discipline that the speculator has. The mechanical system normally includes money management techniques, such as stop-loss orders, which enforce discipline. Traders operating their own fundamental risk assessment analysis often have the tendency to allow losses to run further than is prudent.

A mechanical system establishes a quit point, taking into account profitable and losing situations. The legendary American trader W. D. Gann suggested in his books that positions be quit as soon as the broker called for further margins. The rationale behind this advice was that it was best to quit a losing trade, find out why the trade went wrong, and incorporate the findings in a well-defined rule for the next trade. (Gann was a great believer in stop-loss orders.) A system as intolerant as Gann's calls for well-planned and executed entry points and probably enforces slightly more discipline than novice speculators can absorb.

A mechanical system is usually based on technical analysis of markets, whereas a plan of continuing assessment of the risk/reward possibilities has its basis in fundamental analysis.

There are a huge number of strategies based on fundamental analysis of markets. Many commodities traders and financial dealers will have little to do with technical factors and rely on their own experience and judgment of market fundamentals. I am the first to recognize that fundamental strategies can succeed. This was the basis of trading by the Japanese wool merchant firm that introduced me to futures markets. The intelligence network of this company and skill of its general manager meant that its speculation (euphemistically called "wool trading") was highly successful.

If the speculator has the knowledge, a fundamental strategy can be included as part of his or her policy, particularly if the choice of markets is limited.

My policy choice is for a wide universe of markets, so for me fundamental strategies are inappropriate. I simply do not have the detailed knowledge of the number of markets that I monitor daily. My strategy has to be based on technical analysis to enable me to cover many varied markets whose only common denominator is leveraged price movement.

I shall outline features of technical analysis in the next chapter, and in later chapters produce some recommended strategies and tactics based on technical analysis. There are countless technical strategies available on computer systems, including those "black box" programs which give buying and selling signals without any need to comprehend the reasons behind the calculations.

All readers are no doubt aware of the existence of large-scale computer "program trading," which is mentioned in Wall Street reports from time to time. Maybe, like me, readers have also realized that these computer programs appear only to sell, because the Dow always seems only to fall due to computer program selling. When the Dow rises, the media and spin doctors pronounce that it is due to the advancement of the economy and other positive fundamental factors that computer programs seem to miss!

Whatever the strategy or strategies chosen, the speculator needs to be comfortable in their operation within the trading plan, so as to include it in policy.

If, at this stage of the book, I have succeeded in convincing the

Personal Policy Example

1. Capital of U.S. $100,000 allows multiple contracts in most markets.
2. Computer analysis allows trading tactics to be calculated in 2 hours daily, including strategy calculations on weekends.
3. In most instances markets cannot be closely monitored, so orders must be placed before market opening, and reliance placed on stops.
4. Computer system is designed to identify best potential market of 40 international markets with sufficient volume and volatility.
5. Policy goal is to produce a minimum 50% return on capital by participating in long trend runs, keeping losses below initial margin, and allowing exponential returns.
6. Available equity is calculated on cash balance less current margins. Positive margins will not be included in available equity. Individual market positions will vary from 3% to 12% of available equity. Under exceptional circumstances 24% available equity might be risked in a single market.
7. Cash balance is maintained in U.S. dollars but should be hedged when the dollar is weak, preferably separately from any currency speculation.
8. When available time does not allow analysis as per item 2 above, all market positions should be quit.

Box 2-4.

reader that speculation is not for him or her, then I shall still be content. Gambling and spasmodic speculation for excitement can provide much enjoyment for those who can afford it. I do not seek to curb this enjoyment. It is the losing trades of gamblers which provide the profits to serious speculators. It is serious speculators who enjoy lasting success.

It is to those who are serious about obtaining sustainable profits from speculating in the markets that I say, read on.

3
Technical Analysis: Charts of the Markets

The importance of a sound speculative policy cannot be stressed enough, even to professionals who have already formulated their trading strategies. Before the policy is complete, the less experienced speculator will still have to put together a strategy which suits her or his resources and goals. Every trader must decide whether the basis of the strategy is fundamental or technical analysis.

Fundamental Analysis

A strategy based on fundamental analysis will include knowledge of basic economic concepts, and a technique to utilize a great amount of data to forecast movement of commodities and financial instruments.

The "efficient market hypothesis" developed in the 1960s is based on the premise that the market assimilates all publicly available information quickly and efficiently. Only new information which cannot be predicted will move markets. If new information entering an efficient market cannot be predicted, then the future course of that market also cannot be predicted. The random nature of efficient markets suggested that prices move in a "random walk." Classic economic theory suggests that there is no other way to beat the markets than to obtain information faster than anyone else.

Academic economists still hold a strong belief in the efficient market hypothesis, despite recent work suggesting to the contrary and the poor performance over the years of mathematical economic models. It is my belief that the academic discipline of economics gained strength in the nineteenth century, when the academic discipline of physics was enjoying much success as a result of the industrial revolution. The belief that mathematical models provide early new information on the economy owes much to reliance on the laws of physics.

Market economists are more sanguine in their search for new information than their academic counterparts. They also use mathematical models, but consciously try to gauge the practical factors of government will, political moods, international trends, etc., which are difficult to model.

Fundamental analysts try to weigh up a great deal of information from publicly available statistics. (See the list in Box 3-1.) All of the factors in Box 3-1 are interrelated to some degree. Academic and government economists are continually devising computer models with varying degrees of each factor to forecast a country's economy. The success of these models has been limited, which is a comment either on the complications of fundamental analysis or on the techniques of economists.

In the 1980s and 1990s in particular, there is much anticipation of how others will interpret news of events. Each participant in the market knows that it is not individual opinions that move markets, but the opinion of the majority of traders. The economist J. M. Keynes in the 1930s likened the situation to a newspaper's pick-the-picture-of-the-pretty-girl contest, where the prizes are given not to the readers who correctly assess who is the most beautiful girl, but to those who correctly guess the girl who receives the most votes.

Certainly, analysis of financial instruments is more complicated than judgment of supply/demand factors of other commodities, which is already quite difficult. Most traders of futures who rely solely on fundamental analysis depend heavily on

Fundamental Factors

Commodity supply
Commodity demand
Government loan requirements
Government political pressure on interest rates
Government pressure on bank liquidity
Business cash demand and money supply
Banks' ability to change overdraft rates
Overseas interest rates
Tax payment periods
Economic cyclical indicators
Balance of payments
Export activity
Import activity
Overseas commodities prices
House construction
Weather conditions
Strength or weakness of overseas currencies
Inflation or cost-of-living index
Unemployment

Box 3-1.

media reports, hearsay, brokers' advice, and bank information, and/or have close connections with the trade. Many stockbrokers and dealers in the short-term money and foreign exchange markets follow the latest electronic news and local rumors, taking action to anticipate other traders for short-term profits. Many fundamental analysts, however, also tend to trade for the longer term, often committing funds for 12 months to take advantage of major trends.

There are, no doubt, many successful strategies based on fundamental analysis. My preference for a technical strategy simply suits my own need for a quantifiably disciplined approach. You, the speculator, will have to choose your own approach. I do place some importance on fundamental analysis in tactics—the implementation of strategy—which will be covered in later chapters.

Technical Analysis

The fundamentalist uses the supply/demand equation to deduce the price movement of financial instrument values. The technical analyst contends that this is a futile procedure. The technician asserts that even if the fundamentalist can reason the correct answers to her questions, she cannot be sure that she has answered all the questions, or even asked the right questions. The technician believes that all factors, known and unknown, come together in the marketplace and that the action of the market itself is the best indication of its true course.

The technical analyst does not say that markets are inefficient in acting on available information, but that there is a variety of available information and that diverse conclusions can be drawn from the same information. A market can become overpriced because, acting on the same information, traders anticipate that a trend will continue. A turning point will occur, not from new information, but because an increasing number of traders decide to take profits because they are uncomfortable about the dizzy heights. The action of a few nonrelated individuals soon has an effect on the crowd, whose selling action precipitates a fall. This is not information-based activity but activity based on crowd psychology.

I shall mention more on crowd psychology later in this chapter, but here it is enough to state my opinion that technical analysis is an attempt to chart the flow of the mood of the crowd. From models constructed with statistical information on price, trading volume, futures open interest, etc., the technical analyst tries to identify the patterns of current crowd behavior to compare with recorded patterns, and thus to predict future crowd behavior and movement in price. There have been countless books published on technical analysis since the Dow Theory on general market trends was outlined in *The Wall Street Journal* in the 1890s. Very few of these books mention crowd psychology, but I believe that the success of technical analysis in forecasting crowd behavior is the common hidden factor behind the myriad of charting techniques used to chart the markets.

The technician attempts to chart what has happened in past market movement, and what is happening now in the market, as a guide to what will happen in the future. To do this, she or he follows certain basic premises:

- Market price movements usually follow trends.
- Market price movements will react or rally as prices enter the price zones which previously saw active trading.
- Market price movements form recognizable patterns or chart formations which enable predictions of future movements.

Charts, which are a visual record of price movements, make possible recognition of trends, support and resistance zones, and patterns. Technical analysis of charts is not a science, but an art of considerable depth and complexity. Of the books on charting which are available to help those wishing to trade to a technical plan, the most important for pattern recognition is *Technical Analysis of Stock Trends* by Robert D. Edwards and John Magee (John Magee, Springfield, Massachusetts, 35th printing 1991). First published in 1948, the book is in its sixth edition, and, although it discusses U.S. stock markets, is one of the most comprehensive texts on charting and chart patterns for any market.

> *Even those market authorities who pretend to scorn charts and "chartists" utterly, are not oblivious to the "action" chronicled by the ticker tape, nor do they conceal their respect for the Dow Theory which, whether they realise it or not, is in its very essence purely technical.*
>
> ROBERT D. EDWARDS, 1948

Box 3-2.

A modern standard text for futures traders is John J. Murphy's *Technical Analysis of Futures Markets.* The more statistically minded might appreciate *Smarter Trading* by Perry. J. Kaufman. These are just a few of the numerous books available on technical analysis.

I shall not attempt in this chapter to make my reader an expert technical analyst. I am already assuming that you have a basic trading policy and some computer software, so it is likely that you already have some knowledge of technical analysis. Instead I shall cover the basic elements of technical analysis needed for my suggested trading strategies in a manner that the novice can understand. Even experienced technicians might learn from these basics. The "moving-average cluster" is a simple technique that I learned from a colleague twenty years after first studying moving averages.

The Bar Chart

Apart from a basic line chart, the bar chart—also known as a vertical line chart—is the simplest to construct and the most widely used in commodities and securities trading. It takes only minutes to update a bar chart each day and maintain a clear picture of price movements. The bar chart is a standard feature of most technical analysis computer programs.

The bar chart is constructed by plotting the daily trading range and the closing price of a commodity against a scale on the vertical axis of arithmetical chart paper. The horizontal axis represents time, with one division for each trading session. A vertical line is drawn, representing the range between the high and low prices of a futures contract in each period. A horizontal bar is placed on the line to indicate the closing price. On each successive trading period a new line and bar are drawn, giving a cumulative picture of the movement of prices (see Graph 3-1).

The vertical scale has to be chosen so that the price movement is clearly reflected. Divisions which are too small in a market of low volatility will produce a picture that is hard to read. An overly large scale in an active market will produce a chart that is too big and unwieldy. Graph 3-1(*a*) uses 1 square equivalent to 1

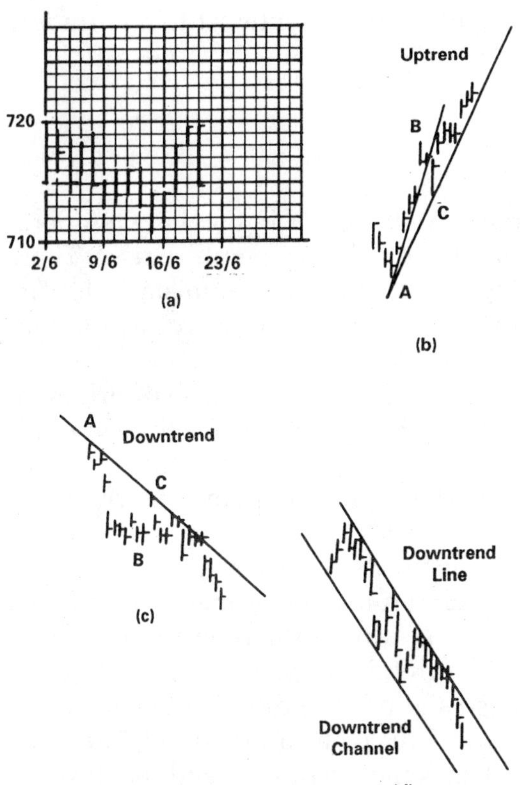

Graph 3-1. The simple bar chart.

index point (10 futures points), which can be considered a moderate scale for a market such as the S&P 500 futures.

The horizontal time scale chosen can be daily (the most common for commodities and financial markets), weekly, or monthly, depending on the use of the chart. A daily chart is necessary for traders who have to take immediate action when circumstances change. A monthly chart is used most often to illustrate history or to project long-range price movements. A quarterly chart provides the best guidance for major trends.

Professional traders have computer systems which instantly capture the price of each trade. Tick bar charts on computer screens can show open/high/low/close at five-minute or hourly intervals; this information is of particular interest to day traders or scalpers.

Trendlines

A familiar example of a trend can be found in the daily temperature. As spring begins, the average daily temperature rises. There may be occasional cold snaps, but the trend is unmistakable. The general tendency of temperatures is to move upwards as summer approaches.

A market trend is the general or prevailing course of prices. In the normal wave motion of a futures price across a chart, a minimum of two points is needed to draw a simple trendline. I do not pay much attention to a trend that has fewer than three points. A fourth point on or close to the trend will confirm it.

Trends may be up, down, or in sideways consolidation. They may be brief (minor) or long-term (major or primary). Trendlines are drawn *under* the prices in an uptrend and *above* prices in a downtrend. In the case of an uptrend (Graph 3-1(*b*)), prices move up from point A to point B, so a minor trendline can be drawn. A reaction from point B to point C breaks the minor trend, but a further rise from point C establishes the major up-trendline through points A and C. In the case of a downtrend (Graph 3-1(*c*)), the major trend drawn through points A and C is confirmed when prices move lower than point B.

"The trend is your friend" runs a trading maxim, meaning that speculative positions should be taken only with the trend. Bought positions are taken with uptrends, sold positions are established in downtrends. Another way of judging trends is by moving averages, which are discussed later in this chapter.

> *The action of the market itself is the best indication of its future course.*
>
> CHARLES H. DOW

Box 3-3.

Trend Channels

Prices rarely move for any length of time in one direction without a corrective shift in the opposite direction. These countermoves are known as reactions against an uptrend, and rallies against a downtrend. Major waves in one direction and smaller counterwaves can create trend channels within parallel trendlines, as illustrated in Graph 3-1(*d*).

Some markets regularly form trend channels which can be used as trading guides. Positions taken at the extremes of the trendline are liquidated when the prices have moved to the opposite extreme of the trend channel.

Support and Resistance

Market positions are taken at price levels which traders consider attractive. For every buyer, there must be a seller. If a number of traders act at certain levels, price congestion patterns of support and resistance are created. If the price rises from a congestion level and then falls, many who had initially sold could be expected to buy back on the return to the original level. The potential buying creates a support area. Conversely, resistance is a price range where selling could develop to stem rising prices.

Support and resistance levels are important in that they can become staging areas for changes in trend. Alternatively, once a support or a resistance area is broken it can then become the reverse congestion area. In Graph 3-2, a resistance/support area is around 105.50 ($105^{16}/_{32}$). The market initially peaked in January 1992 at 105.34, which became resistance which would not be clearly broken in August–October 1992, which saw a trading range of 102.91–106.62. That resistance range was clearly broken in February 1993 in the surge to the 1993 peak. The same range then formed a support area in April 1994. After the trough in November 1994, the bull market again ran into resistance at 105.31 in March 1995. The break of resistance in May 1995 led to a strong surge of interest rate euphoria.

Many analysts will not take a position in the market until major support and resistance areas have been penetrated.

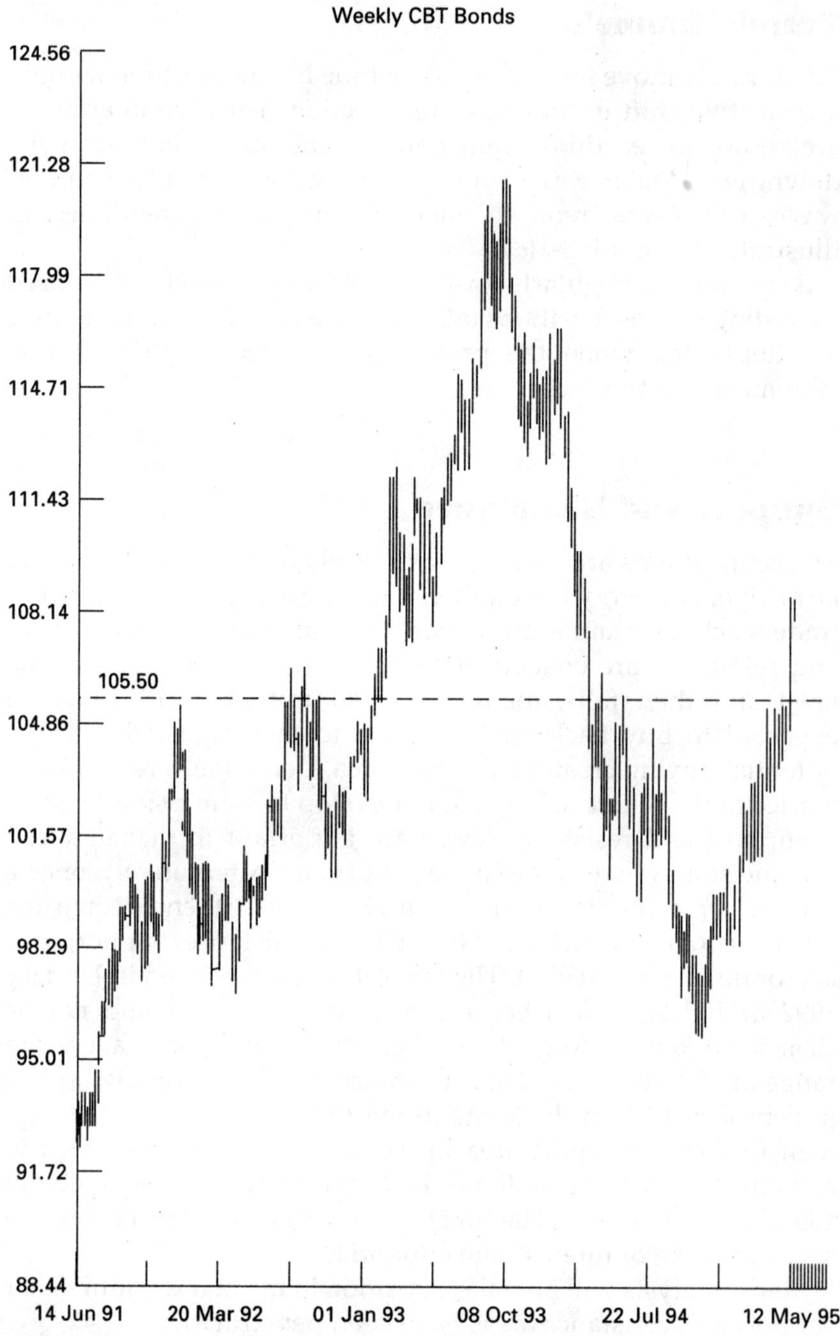

Graph 3-2. A price breakthrough T-Bond resistance area.

Let's look at another market example before moving on. In Graph 3-3, the NZFE40 monthly bar chart, support congestion was formed in the 2085–1750 area from which the August 1989 rally was mounted. The congestion was broken on the downside in March 1990 and the subsequent rally could not exceed the previous support congestion, which then became resistance congestion against further rises. After a temporary up break in early 1994 the congestion again became a support area into 1995.

Angle Lines

The legendary William Gann (see Box 3-4) placed great store in angular lines drawn from major peaks and troughs. He suggested that prime angles of 82.5°, 75°, 63.75°, 45°, 26.25°, 15°, and 7.5° might indicate significant turning points, particularly when combined with his time and price calculations. His theories are complicated, but I have found some simple applications helpful.

W. D. Gann

I expect to continue to learn something every year as long as I live. Observations and keen comparisons of past market movements will reveal what commodities are going to do in the future, because the future is but a repetition of the past.

W. D. GANN, 1942

A legendary figure in the field of technical analysis was William D. Gann (1878–1955), who developed a combination of mathematical, geometric, and astrological principles for methodical trading. Gann was particularly keen on the relationships of anniversaries of past price peaks and troughs, and their respective time relationships. His theories are much too complex to explain in a single chapter, but serious analysts could look for his books, republished by Lambert-Gann Publishing Co. Inc. (Pomeroy, Washington 99347).

Box 3-4.

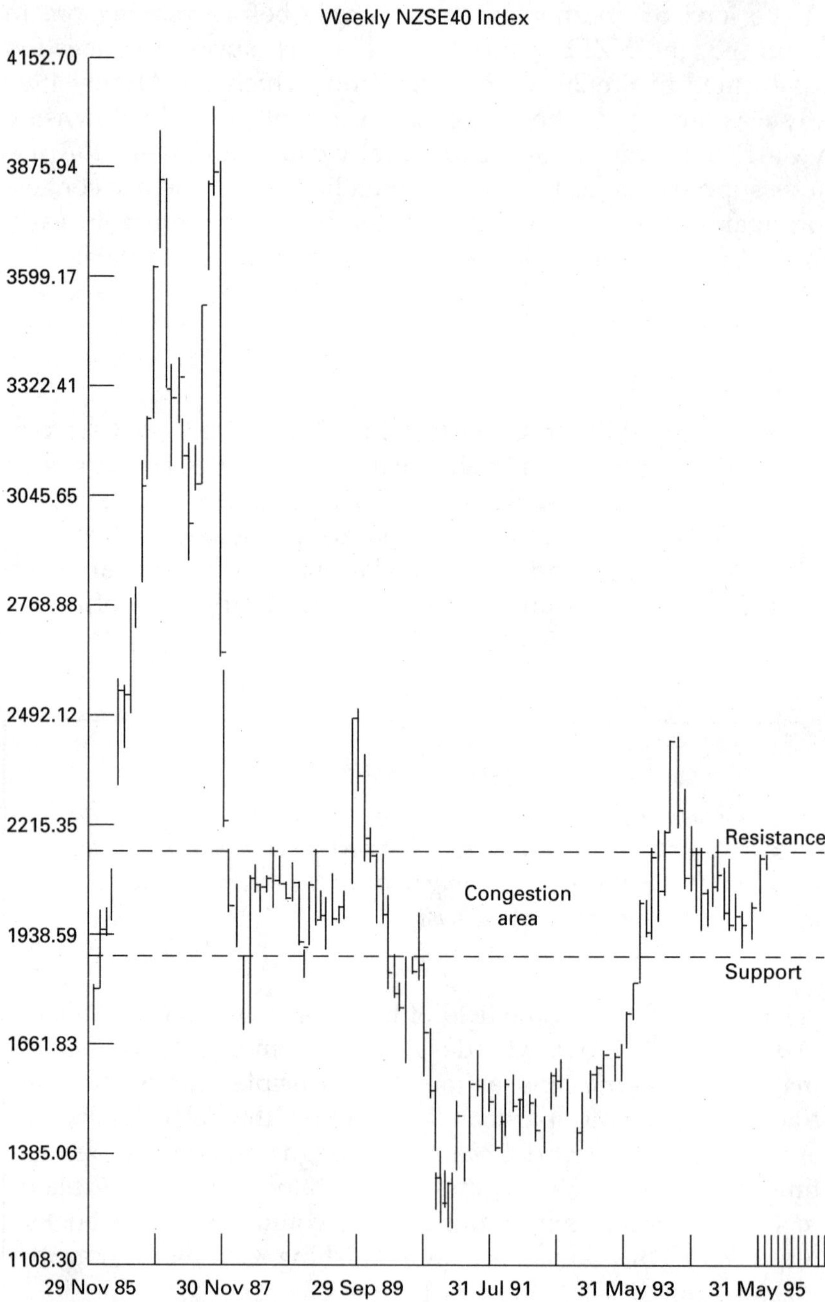

Graph 3-3. New Zealand stocks congestion area.

Gann's theory was that the natural movement of markets was at a pace where price movement equaled time movement. Thus a commodity or stock would move away from a major trough in equal increments of time and price, or, if the increments were disparate, would return to the natural 1 × 1 line or 45° angle.

I use a 45° trend from a major top or major bottom on a monthly chart to determine the perfect trend of the major market movement. As a rule of thumb, when the market is rising or falling at an angle sharper than 45°, then it is becoming more speculative. I can then move to the weekly chart to examine the 45° trend from the most recent intermediate top or bottom, and if necessary I can move to daily or even intraday charts.

When speculating, I am most comfortable in the time period in which the market trend approximates 45°. A market in which the major trend is less than 45° is underperforming and could be more suited to investment than speculation. A market in which the major trend is faster than 62.5° is attractive to speculators. An upward exponential curve is the sign of a major boom, which must be treated with great care as the trend tries to approach 90°. The explosive growth that occurs in the last stages of an exponential curve generally signals the termination of the major bull trend, in a not dissimilar way to that demonstrated by one of nature's examples of exponential growth—cancer.

Graph 3-4 pictures the practically exponential movement in cotton from the 1986 trough which then corrected back to the 45° angle line in 1988. In 1995 the highest cotton prices since the U.S. Civil War touched the 45° angle line from the 1986 trough, which suggests that a peak price will be reached in 1995–1996, and also suggests the possibility that it will not be seen again for many years.

Graph 3-4 also illustrates the speculative opportunities from sharp, sustained trend rises.

Elliot Wave Theory

The simple, oft-repeated adage of trading with the trend can prove to be simplistic in the marketplace. For instance, the conservative trader who waits for three points on a trend to confirm

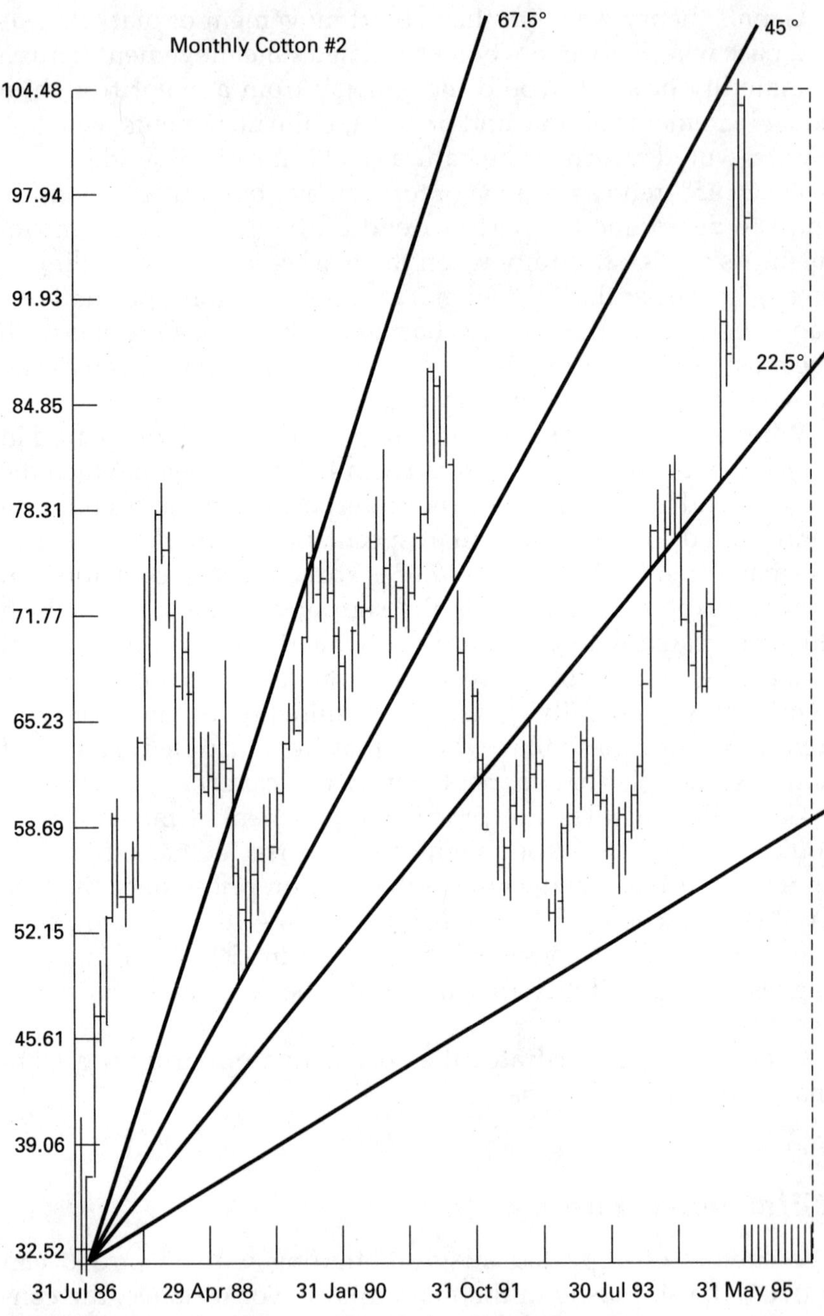

Graph 3-4. Gann angles on New York cotton.

an entry point might find that he or she is entering the market just prior to a change of direction. It would be helpful to know whether the trend had some way to go before committing money to the marketplace.

In the 1930s R. N. Elliot formulated the wave theory which bears his name, and which can be used to forecast the likely course of trend movement. The simple theory that bull markets form five wave patterns, which are followed by a bear correction of three waves, has been made complicated by a number of corollaries to explain the minor exceptions to basic theory. Further studies on Elliot's theories are essential for the serious analyst, but I believe that the trader can make use of Elliot Wave theory by simply recognizing the current wave.

The wave theory states that a market rises in three impulse waves of varying duration, separated by two corrective waves of shorter duration than the impulse waves. These waves are numbered odd for impulse, even for correction, as per Graph 3-5. Once wave 5 has peaked, the market enters its corrective phase of three waves, which are designated by the letters a, b, c. When the corrective phase is complete, the bull run can recommence. Each

R. N. Elliot

In the period 1929–1934 an American management accountant, Ralf Nelson Elliot, examined trading patterns in the U.S. stock market while recovering from a debilitating illness. In 1935 he produced a booklet, "The Wave Principle," describing his theory of the repetitive nature of stock market behavior in that the Dow Jones Industrial Average formed discernible patterns which were repetitive in form, if not necessarily in time or amplitude. Elliot's basic philosophy, later expressed in a book, *Nature's Law—The Secret of the Universe,* was that all bull markets consist of five waves and all bear markets form three waves. This enabled him to forecast the great 1940s bull market. Elliot's theories have been furthered by Robert Prechter, the author of a number of books on Elliot.

Box 3-5.

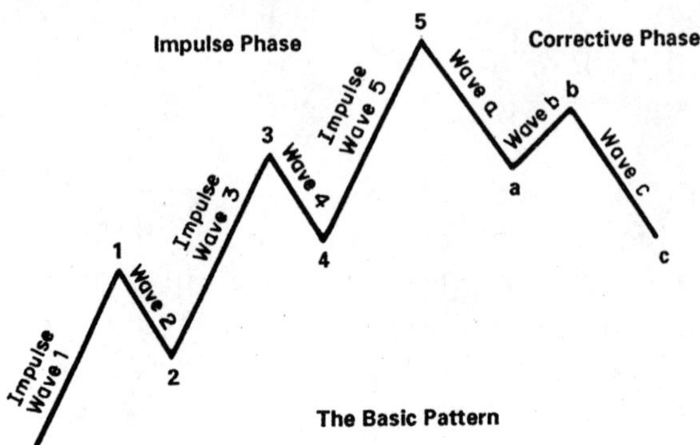

Graph 3-5. The basic Elliot Wave pattern.

wave consists of the same wave pattern of minor waves, and in turn makes up part of a pattern of larger waves. In today's terms, Elliot's theories would come under the umbrella of chaos and fractal theory.

Other basic Elliot characteristics are:

1. One wave of three impulse waves is usually an extended wave, which is often the third impulse wave in financial markets. Commodity markets often enjoy the fifth impulse wave as the extension, which can occur as a mini-boom blow-off wave.
2. Wave 3 cannot be the shortest impulse wave.
3. The extended impulse wave is related mathematically to the other waves, usually 1.618 or 2.618 times the length.
4. When the third impulse wave is the extension, the fifth impulse is often equal to the first wave.
5. When the wave 2 correction is short and simple, wave 4 correction is likely to be longer and more complicated.

Elliot refers to the relationship of one wave to another, which often can demonstrate a ratio such as 1.618 (mentioned in rule 3 above), as theorized by the thirteenth-century mathematician Leonardo Pisano, known as Fibonacci. Working on ancient

Nature and Fibonacci

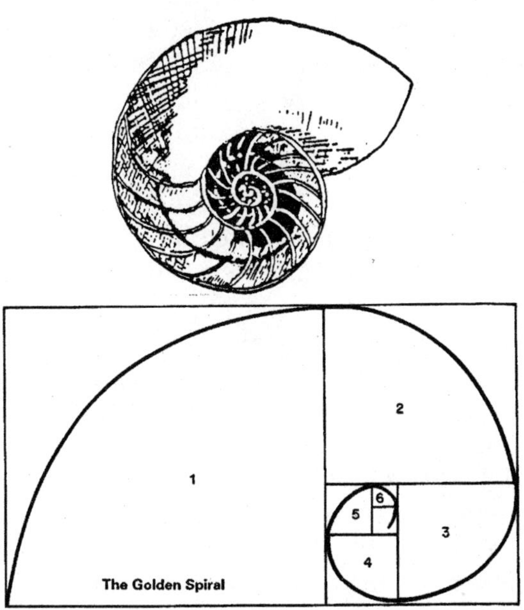

An Italian mathematician, Leonardo of Pisa (da Pisa, or Pisano, 1170–1240), known as Fibonacci, devised a summation series in which each element is the sum of the two preceding figures: 1, 1, 2, 3, 5, 8, 13, 21, 34, 55, 89, 144. The Macmillan *Dictionary of Biography* (3d edition) says that Fibonacci was "the son of a merchant, [and] one of the greatest early writers on arithmetic and algebra. In his *Liber abaci* written around 1202 he introduced the Arabic systems of numerals into Europe; in later works he made highly original applications of algebra to geometry." Fibonacci's summation series has at various times been related to the "golden spiral."

Box 3-6.

Egyptian theory, Fibonacci conceived a numation series which might have been related to the natural spiral found in nature, as the sunflower spiral, leaf arrangement of plants, and even the reproduction rate of rabbits. The Egyptians are said to have consciously employed the Fibonacci ratio in the Great Pyramid of Gizeh, the Greeks in the Parthenon, and Leonardo da Vinci in his art.

As intriguing as is the philosophy of the lasting nature of the ancient Fibonacci series, it is the practical aspect that is helpful to the trader. Each element is approximately 1.618 times the previous number, as a minute with the calculator and the series will show: 1, 1, 2, 3, 5, 8, 13, 21, 34, 55, 89, 144. . . . Simplistically, the trader can recognize the current wave using the Elliot principle, and forecast its peak or trough by theorizing the relationship of the complete wave as a ratio to past waves. One regular target is that the corrective wave 2 can be 0.382 times wave 1 (or 0.5×). The impulse wave 3 can be 1.618 times wave 1 (or 2× or 2.618 or 3×). Impulse wave 5 is often equal to wave 1, or 0.618 times wave 3.

As a trend-following trader, I want to trade Elliot impulse waves 3 and 5, because they are the impulses which are likely to last longest. As a conservative trader, I prefer to avoid trading correction waves 2 and 4.

My above statement that, "simplistically, the trader can recognize the current wave," appreciates that it is indeed far from simple to recognize a wave pattern while it is still forming. Sometimes the trader recognizes the major wave, but is wiped out from a large minor wave correction. Appreciation that Elliot Wave recognition is an art, not a science, is a major reason for my trading strategy based on trend following. Entry and exits are signaled by objective methods, even though the wave pattern might influence the size of the speculative position.

My recognition of the current Elliot Wave has been enhanced since I applied crowd psychology rationale to market movements. The first impulse wave is born following a long trend move in the other direction. The crowd is slow to recognize that a trend is reversing, and often simply acts uncomfortable that momentum is changing. Following a downtrend, some astute traders notice the slowing momentum and commence to take profits. This often leads to the triggering of stop-loss signals of other traders, which in turn causes the crowd to start to shift its position. Some in the crowd use the stop-losses as signals to reverse position, and in general the crowd starts to relate to the signs of a rising market. This is the psychology of the first impulse wave.

Not all the crowd is convinced that the major movement has reversed. There were traders looking to sell who were waiting for a rally such as this to enter the market. These traders, often hedgers, sell the market on the first sign of weakness in wave 1. The market weakens further and triggers sell signals of short-term speculators. The crowd has not yet gained enough confidence to hold long positions in the face of what looks like professional selling for the resumption of the downtrend. The crowd quits longs, and some even reverse positions. This is my explanation of the thinking behind corrective wave 2.

A fundamental factor might enter the market to cut wave 2 short. It might have been this factor that bullish insiders knew would cause the major trend to change. A reasonable target for wave 2 is 0.382 or 0.5 times wave 1.

If the correction continues past the halfway point of wave 1, the major low point of wave 1 becomes a target for those now committed to a falling market. Many in the crowd, having lost money in the last move, will want to add to short positions once prices move below the low. However, this low point might be particularly attractive to hedgers and market professionals who believe that it was a major trend turning point. Buyers start to slow the down move and then it is reversed above the previous low at a level maybe around 0.8 times wave 1. This causes the crowd to scramble for cover. Stop-losses, reverses, and fresh buying can cause an explosion upward that shows up on the charts as a "double bottom" or "W" shape. Corrective wave 2 has finished and impulse wave 3 has started.

The high point of wave 2 then becomes a target point. There might be some minor corrective action around the target, but once the point has been exceeded the crowd gathers confidence that the major trend is indeed now up. More long positions are added. Buyers become more aggressive than sellers, and the trend gains strength. The crowd should be able to sustain a rise 1.618 times the length of wave 1. In most stock and financial futures markets, wave 3 is the dominant wave of the trend. In some commodity markets wave 5 is the longest.

Waves 4 and 5 often follow the same nervous sentiment as waves 1 and 2, except that they are topping formations in a bull market. If wave 3 has been consistent, the crowd's confidence has grown, as has the size of the crowd, because late starters have joined. If the size of the crowd of buyers becomes too large, the number of sellers becomes scarce. The scarcity of sellers can cause a sharp move at the top of wave 3 known as a "blow-out top." Sellers suddenly abound and the market reverses sharply to commence corrective wave 4.

Wave 3 often dies of exhaustion, and profit taking and minor loss taking can cause the turn. If the crowd is particularly smug, the corrective wave 4 might only be short-lived, because waiting in the wings have been those looking for a correction to add to long positions. These buyers calm the nerves of the crowd, and even encourage further "me too" buying to stimulate the last impulse wave 5.

Wave 5 can start confidently but fade fast once it has exceeded the wave 3 major high. In many ways 5 is the easiest wave to pick because the length of previous waves can give good targets to those who have studied Elliot. Even knowing that the market is in its last stages of a trend can allow for caution, if one is not simply part of the amorphous crowd.

In my privateer analogy, the charts and wave patterns can be like ancient maps which one knows contain many errors and false entries. By knowing the psychology of the mapmaker, one might determine which are the false entries. The market mapmaker is the amorphous crowd, and many times when looking at chart patterns I have pondered the above psychology in conjunction with the waves to determine the true position.

Waves don't keep in the same regular formation as the schematic in Graph 3-5. Graph 3-6 is an illustration of one interpretation of the Elliot waves of IBM in 1994. My privateer strategy seeks to be long in wave 3 and wave 5, but in wave 4, IBM would have provided some shorting opportunities.

My privateer strategy in the following chapter is designed for early entry into an expansion wave, accepting that at times the trade might need to be quit early because the initial signal was false. Elliot wave recognition will not change that strategy but might marginally alter the number of contracts or shares in a single trade.

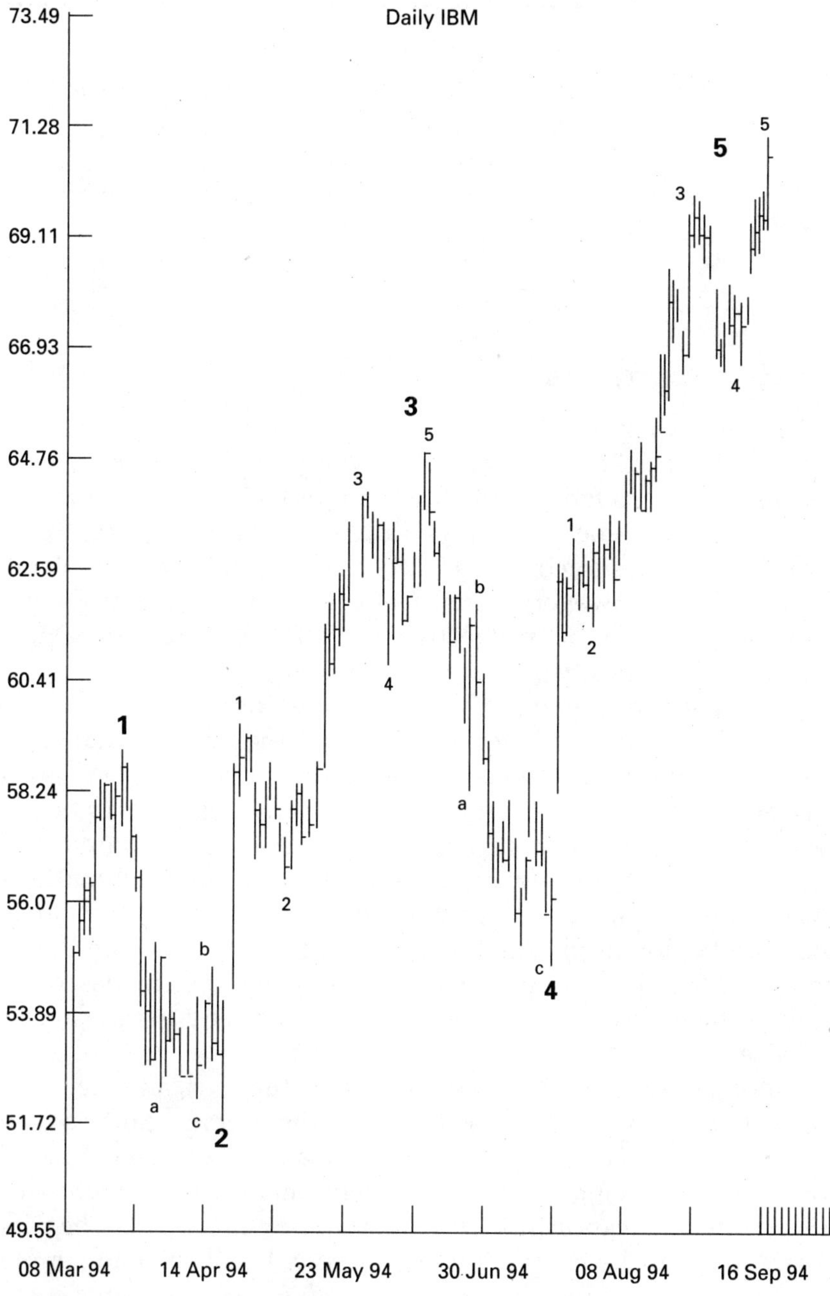

Graph 3-6. Elliot Waves of IBM stock.

> *The world's "ships of state" did not just have faulty compasses, they had no compasses, inadequate speed logs and little real idea of where they had been and where they were bound.*
>
> U.S. CHIEF STATISTICIAN DR. JOSEPH DUNCAN, 1993

Box 3-7.

Moving Averages

The price movement of commodities and financial instruments at times ebbs and flows erratically. Many traders make losses because they respond to daily fluctuations by jumping in and out of the market. Trendlines can be drawn on charts and chart patterns can be observed to formulate successful trading plans. Many traders, however, do not feel comfortable with subjective decision making. A more objective view of the market can be provided mathematically by moving averages.

I have been testing and discarding different technical analysis methods since 1965. I have now reached the opinion that forecasting techniques produce reliable results only when one looks forward in weeks and months. Accordingly, I use chart pattern recognition, Elliot Wave theory, and Gann price/time and cyclical techniques to forecast likely movements in financial markets over those time spans. Forecasts cannot be 100% correct; at times they can be downright disastrous. To allow for the possibility of being wrong, I developed a trend-following system based on moving averages which keeps to a minimum any losses caused by false forecasting.

Averages of prices smooth out daily fluctuations, and, depending on the number of days used to strike the average, can produce a gently undulating trendline. There are a number of methods of formulating moving averages: conventional, average modified, weighted, and exponentially smoothed. Each of them has its champions. In the chapters which follow, I will refer to simple moving averages for the more relaxed strategic trading, and exponential moving averages for active tactical entries and exits.

Moving Averages Need Not Be Simple

A moving average can smooth out the daily fluctuations, and, according to the number of days which make up the average, can produce a gentle undulating line. There are a number of methods of formulating moving averages. The types of moving averages are:

Simple, which is calculated by adding the daily prices for the number of days required, and dividing the sum by the number of days. The n average for each subsequent day is made by deducting the price for day $n - 1$ from the aggregate, adding today's value, and dividing by n.

Modified, for which one deducts the moving average instead of the daily price $n - 1$.

Weighted, which adds weight to recent data to make averages more relevant to today's market.

Exponentially smoothed, which uses a World War II mathematical technique for tracking aircraft and projecting their position by geometric progression.

These are all fully described in Perry Kaufman's book *Commodity Trading Systems and Methods.*

Box 3-8.

A *simple moving average* is calculated by adding the daily prices for the number of days required, and dividing the sum by the number of days. If a 3-day moving average is required and the first, second, and third day's prices are 50, 51, and 52 respectively, their average is 50 + 51 + 52 (total 153) divided by 3, which equals 51. If the price on the fourth day is 53, it is added to the previous aggregate, bringing the aggregate to 206, and the first-day price (50) is subtracted, to arrive at the new total of 156, which in turn is divided by 3 to obtain the new moving average of 52. The same procedure is followed to reach the moving average of any number of days, as can be seen in Box 3-9, showing the

Hang Seng moving averages, December 1991

Daily close	5-day aggreg.	5-day avg.	10-day aggreg.	10-day avg.	20-day aggreg.	20-day avg.
4157.2	20 688	4137.5	41 678	4167.8	84 016	4200.8
4190.0	20 728	4145.5	41 625	4162.5	83 970	4198.5
4203.2	20 837	4167.3	41 608	4160.8	83 942	4197.1
4128.3	20 841	4168.1	41 534	4153.4	83 818	4190.9
4097.2	20 776	4155.2	41 452	4145.2	83 674	4183.7
4096.0	20 715	4142.9	41 402	4140.2	83 560	4178.0
4155.5	20 680	4136.0	41 408	4140.8	83 444	4172.2
4171.7	20 649	4129.7	41 485	4148.5	83 416	4170.8
4185.0	20 706	4141.1	41 546	4154.6	83 340	4167.0
4177.7	20 786	4157.2	41 562	4156.2	83 318	4165.9
4182.8	20 873	4174.5	41 587	4158.7	83 266	4163.3
4142.6	20 860	4172.0	41 540	4154.0	83 166	4158.3
4146.1	20 834	4166.8	41 883	4148.3	83 090	4154.1
4192.8	20 842	4168.4	41 547	4154.7	83 082	4154.1
4236.2	20 901	4180.1	41 686	4168.6	83 138	4156.9
4275.2	20 993	4198.6	41 866	4186.6	83 268	4163.4

Box 3-9.

Hong Kong Hang Seng index moving averages in December 1991.

The moving averages can be plotted on a chart as shown in Graph 3-7. In practice, of course, the computer does these calculations, which are standard in most technical analysis software. The daily price movements show some erratic movement, although the trend is noticeably up. The 5-day moving average flows relatively smoothly, close to the daily plot, confirming the short-term uptrend on December 17. The 10-day average is also smooth but further away from the daily plot and did not confirm the uptrend until December 24. The 20-day average is the smoothest but well

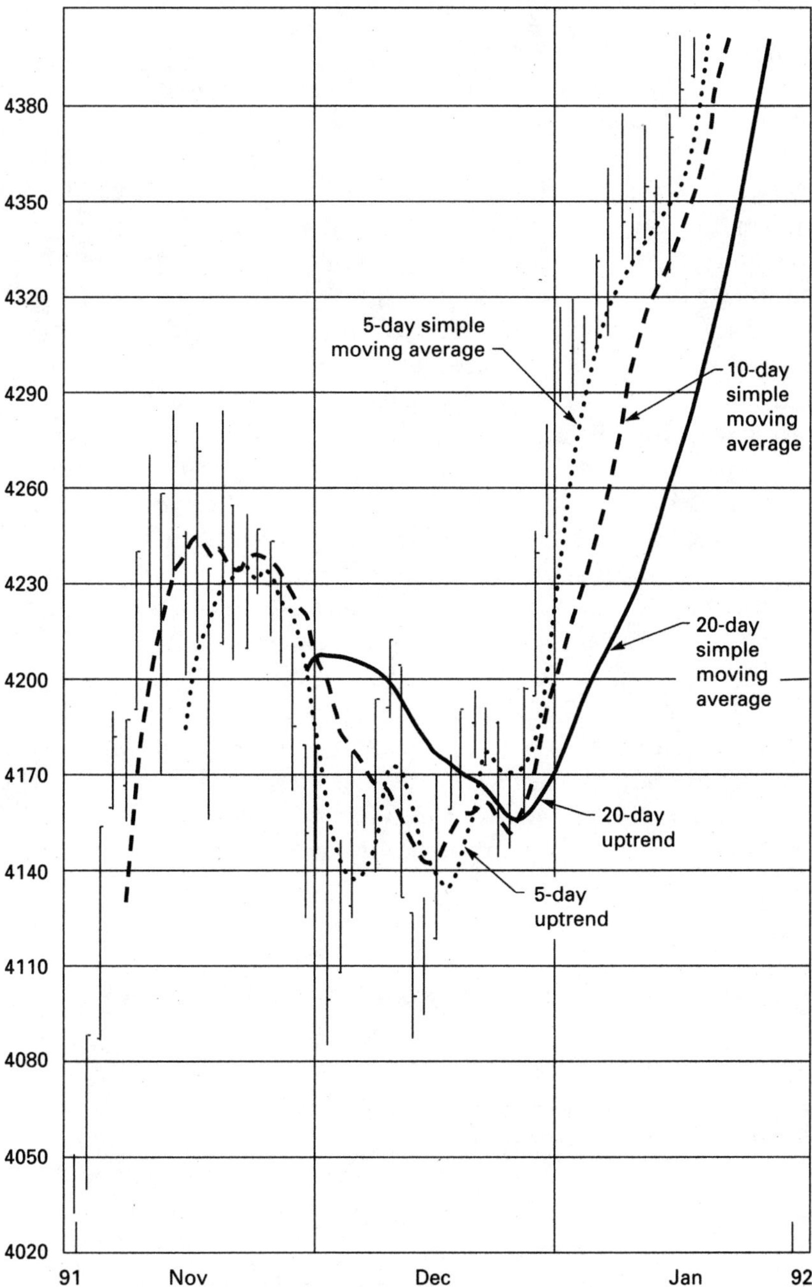

Graph 3-7. Hong Kong Stock Index simple moving averages.

away from the daily plot so that its confirmation of the uptrend did not occur until December 27.

To use another marine analogy, the moving average is as smooth as the wake of a ship. The wake tells us where the ship has been, and gives an indication of the direction the ship intends to take.

Moving averages will always lag behind the daily price. In bull markets this lag will cause the moving average to be below the price; in bear markets it will be above. When prices change direction the daily price will cross through the moving average, possibly giving a trading signal. A buy can be signaled at the point where the rising price passes through the moving average. The crossover where the falling price passes through the moving average can signal a sell.

An *exponential moving average,* or *exponentially smoothed moving average* to use the proper term, is an average where more emphasis is placed on the most recent data by reducing the value of the older data by a constant percentage. I am not a "rocket scientist" and find the formula relatively complicated. In practice I simply rely on the standard calculations which are available in most technical analysis software programs. One formula is shown in Box 3-10, but those who are mathematically minded should seek a full explanation of the use of exponential moving averages from *Commodity Trading Systems and Methods* by Perry J. Kaufman. The action signals for exponential moving averages are the same as the crossing signals for simple moving averages.

Formula for the Exponential Moving Average

$$\text{EMA}_n = Cy + (1 - \text{C})\text{EMA}_{(n-1)}$$

where EMA_n = exponential average on day n

$\text{EMA}_{(n-1)}$ = exponential average yesterday (day $n - 1$)

C = EMA smoothing constant = $2/(s + 1)$

s = simple moving average length

y = price on day n

Box 3-10.

In practice, simple crossing signals could prove as erratic as any other subjective cues. The moving-average proponent tries to avoid erratic trading. Constant buying and selling produces a "whipsaw" effect which must be avoided for profitable trading.

Combination Moving Averages

A number of systems, including lagging and band techniques, avoid the whipsaw effect. Practice shows that the simplest, most successful method is to use two moving averages. The longer the moving-average time span, the less sensitive it is to new daily inputs. As a result, it is slower to signal trend changes. A combination of a relatively sensitive average, reflecting the short-term trend, and a less sensitive average, representing the medium trend, will indicate a change of trend close to the daily movement but sufficiently far away to avoid whipsaw trades.

The moving average composed of the least number of days will cross through the slower moving average composed of the greater number of days, with a further lag behind the daily price. If the correct two moving averages have been chosen, the trading signals should result in the profitable course of cutting losses short and letting profits run. The choice of the two moving averages is particularly important and many studies have been undertaken in this regard. One of the better known is Donchian's 5-day and 20-day simple moving averages, begun in 1961 using volatility-penetration criteria. Donchian personalized the system by adding many judgmental factors relating to the extent to which the 20-day average must be penetrated and the day of the week on which the signals occur.

I maintain that the periods chosen for moving averages depend on the volatility and volume of trading for each market. When a market is quiet, slower averages of extended numbers of days will prove more profitable. An active market will be able to support more frequent trades, so faster averages of shorter durations are often more fruitful. Computer programs are available to calculate moving-average combinations over a period, although they cannot guarantee future profits, even if they have been successful in the past.

From 1965 to 1980, when I tested simple moving averages on wool, a combination of 10-day and 50-day averages proved most successful. In boom periods, particularly in 1972–1973, I switched to 5-day and 20-day averages because the lag of the longer periods was too great.

From 1975 to 1984, when I computerized my system, I used 5-day and 20-day simple averages for cattle, gold, U.S. interest rates, and stock exchange indexes. The volume of Sydney Futures Exchange (SFE) silver and fat-lamb futures was not conducive to technical analysis. In fact, technical analysis is not practical for any market that has low turnover, because the traded prices do not provide any general consensus.

Good results can be obtained from a combination of 5-day and 20-day simple averages in most international financial instrument futures markets.

I have used simple trading signals to buy when the 5-day (or 10-day) moving average rises through the 20-day (or 50-day) moving average, and to sell when the 5-day (or 10-day) moving average falls through the 20-day (or 50-day) moving average. Speculators can thus reverse their positions on each signal and would always be in the market. Buy hedgers will buy futures on a buy signal, and liquidate and be out of the market on a sell signal. Sell hedgers will sell futures on a sell signal, and liquidate and be out of the market on a buy signal.

Graph 3-8 illustrates the movement of the strong Japanese yen against the U.S. dollar on the Chicago Mercantile Exchange International Monetary Market (CME IMM) futures market. The buy signal was the crossover point where the 5-day simple moving average moved above the 20-day average on February 10, when the yen could have been bought at 102.30. The two moving averages stayed apart in a strong rising trend until the 5-day moving average (SMA5) crossed down through the 20-day (SMA20) on May 2, when the yen could have been sold at 120.80. By following these simple buy/sell signals, a profit of $23,125 would have been possible on an initial margin of around $7600. Even allowing for the need for committed funds of 3 times the ini-

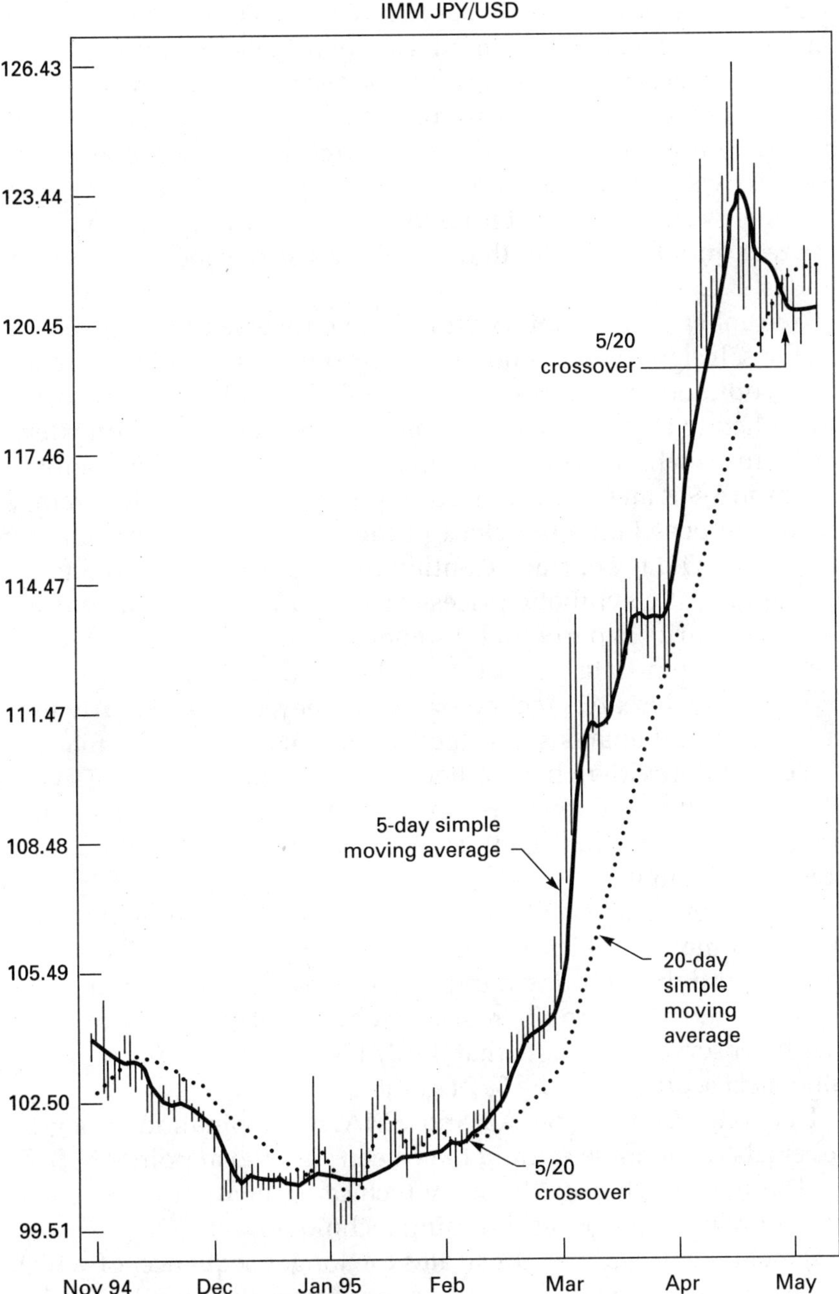

Graph 3-8. Japanese yen combination moving averages.

tial margin, a profit of 101% could have been achieved in 81 days. Such is the treasure which modern-day privateers seek.

The signals occurred above the trough and well below the peak because of the time lag. This simple system was developed by me primarily for hedging, and, even though this example was also speculatively profitable, does not seek to pick peaks and troughs. Moving averages of shorter history would indicate action closer to peaks and troughs, but they are likely also to produce whipsaw trades.

A number of speculators would have reversed their positions on the sell signal. This is not my philosophy, as I shall show later. In my opinion separate decisions should be made on when to exit and when to enter a market. Reversing positions on the one decision causes whiplashes, so should take place only infrequently.

Graph 3-9 is an example of a 3-day and 13-day moving-average system imposed on a bar chart of the Eurodollar futures market perpetual 90-day contract. Continuous or perpetual contracts are mathematically synthetic prices calculated to emulate a contract whose maturity is perpetually some days in the future. Perpetual contracts, from data providers such as CSI Inc. in Boca Raton, Florida, and Research Technology in Sydney, are particularly useful in technical analysis to establish long histories of the market. Other data providers have other forms of continuous data available, but my preference is for perpetual contracts. Technical analysis of individual contract months is necessary for actual trading decisions.

The upper panel (*a*) illustrates a relatively short moving-average combination which I discuss in the next chapter. Three-day (SMA3) and thirteen-day moving averages (SMA13) are the closest that I like to get to the market from a strategic point of view. Astute observers will note that the 3/13 combination is the earlier Fibonacci sequence to the 5/21 combination.

Had one used the SMA3 and SMA13 combination to signal reversals, small losses would have been suffered at points A, B, C, D. These were whipsaw losses, which cause many traders to discard moving averages as a trading technique.

Panel (*b*) of Graph 3-9 illustrates the longer sequence, of which I am fond—the 5/20-day. It can be noted that in the period January–May 1995 only one whipsaw, point A, occurred.

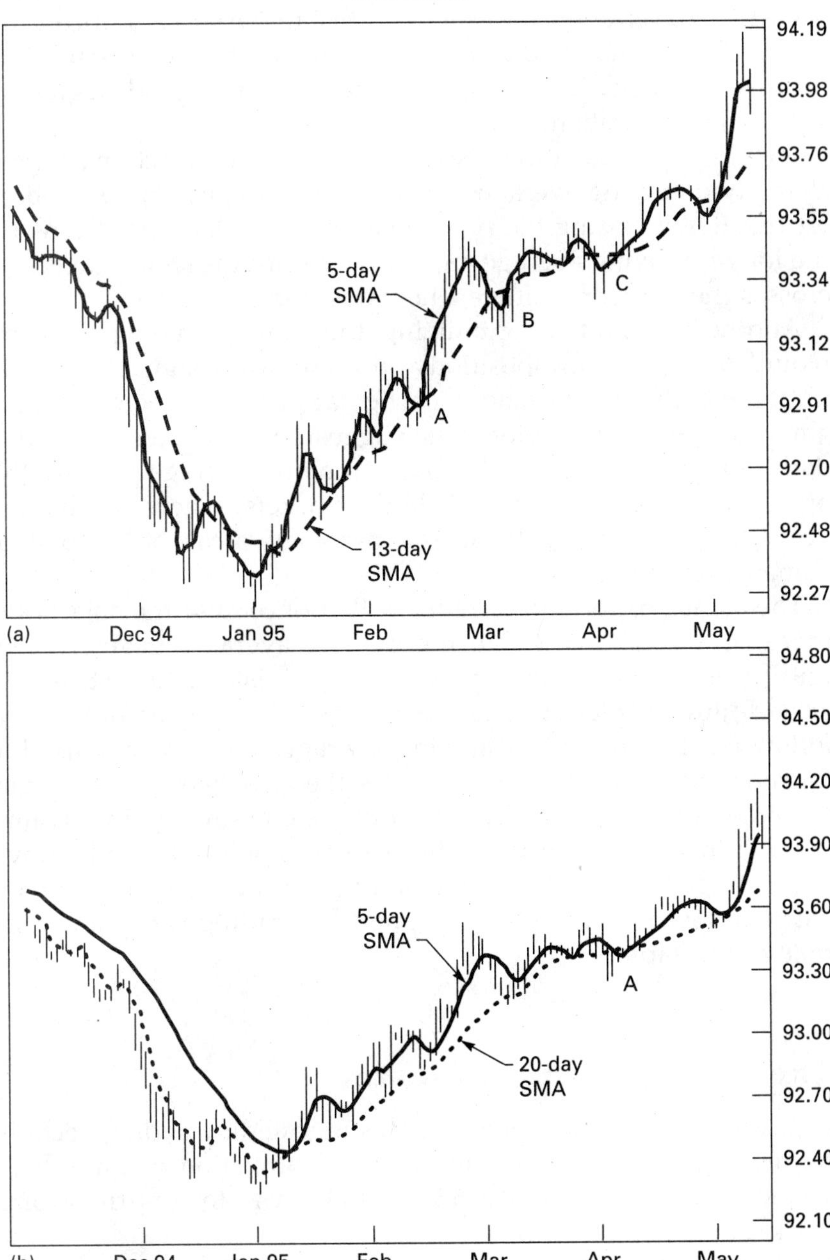

Graph 3-9. Eurodollar moving average.

Only trial and error can show which combination of averages is best for the circumstances. I can attest to the success since 1978 of the 5-day and 20-day combination on the SFE's bank-bill futures contracts. Recent research has shown a good degree of success in other financial markets.

For ease of explanation I have mentioned taking action as soon as the two moving averages cross. Speculators might obtain better results by closing the positions when the daily price crosses the longer moving average and waiting until the shorter average crosses the longer to initiate a new position.

Another method of optimizing the moving-average system would be to quit any positions on a crossover signal and wait until the daily price reaches a particular parameter before taking a new speculative position. One suggested parameter is that the daily price should exceed the longer moving-average price by 1% of the daily price. In more volatile markets, where results are downgraded by whipsaw losses, parameters can be calculated using historical data.

The astute, experienced trader will at once raise the objections that one doesn't know that the moving averages have crossed until after the day's trading session is finished. In fact, many trend followers place orders for action on the opening of the day following the time when moving averages cross. I have used a formula (Box 3-11) which calculates the crossover point on the same day that it occurs. By calculating a crossover point of simple-moving-average *highs* or the crossover point of simple-moving-average *lows,* one has a stop point to be entered on the day for entry and exit. Use of this stop point for trading is explained in following chapters.

The Moving-Average Cluster

A further moving-average method, suggested by Sydney technical analyst Dawn Bolton-Smith, is a combination of three harmonic moving averages—5, 15, and 30 days—to confirm strong market movement.

A cluster occurs when the simple moving averages 5-day, 15-day, 30-day (a harmonic progression) all cross within a few days

Moving-Average Crossover Formula

By calculating the potential crossover point of simple moving averages on either the daily *highs* or daily *lows,* the point at which a stop order can be placed is obtained, to be triggered when the market reaches that *high* or *low* point on the same day.

$$\text{Crossover point} = \frac{x[\Sigma_y - AGO_{(y+1)}] - y[\Sigma_x + AGO_{(x+1)}]}{y - x}$$

Formula for 3/13 Period Crossover

$$\text{Crossover point} = \frac{3[\Sigma_{13} - AGO_{14}] - 13[\Sigma_3 + AGO_4]}{13 - 3}$$

$$= 0.3[\Sigma_{13} - AGO_{14}] - 1.3[\Sigma_3 + AGO_4]$$

where x = periods in short average
y = periods in long average
$AGO_{(x+1)}$ = price at $(x + 1)$ periods ago
$AGO_{(y+1)}$ = price at $(y + 1)$ periods ago
Σ_x = aggregate of prices for x periods
Σ_y = aggregate of prices for y periods

Box 3-11.

of each other. Graph 3-10 illustrates a NASDAQ stock, Maxus Energy, in which a cluster occurred on November 10 providing a strong sell signal at $4\frac{15}{64}$. The buyback signal occurred on the 5/15 crossover on January 24 prior to a sharp lift in the market from $3\frac{15}{64}$. A confirmed buy signal occurred when the SMA15 and SMA30 crossed on January 30 to form a loose cluster. The loose cluster signal preceded the takeover offer announced on February 28.

The main combinations of moving averages mentioned have been multiples of five (5, 10, 15, 20, 30, 50). This is partly because,

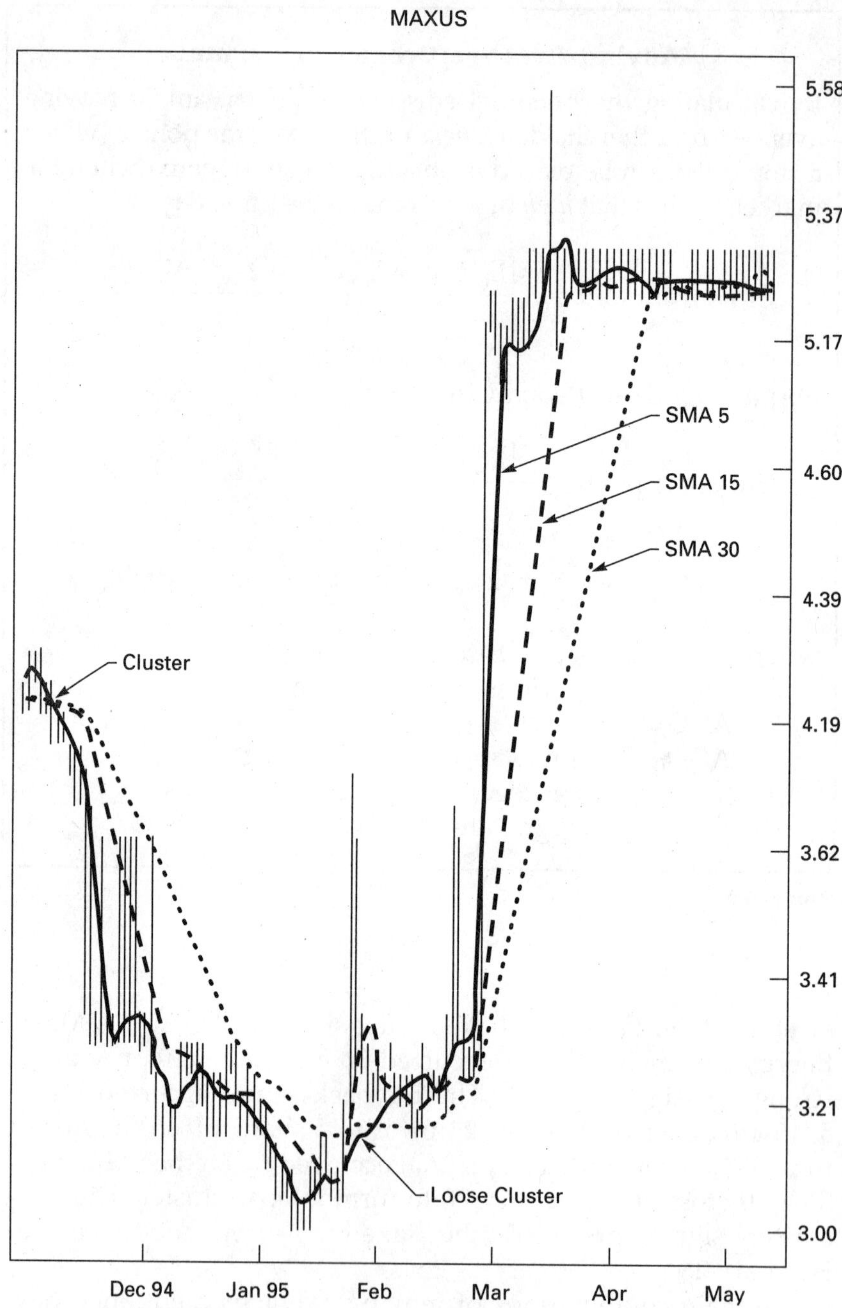

Graph 3-10. Moving average clusters before Maxus takeover.

before computers, calculations were carried out by hand or using calculators. In recent years I have been inclined to experiment with combinations of averages based on the Fibonacci sequence.

The results I have observed in the 5/20-day combinations in interest rates may well be incidental to their proximity to the Fibonacci combination 5/21 (ratio 0.238). It may also be that better results would be obtained using a 13/55 (ratio 0.236) combination rather than 10/50-day periods. As you will see in the next chapter, by using synergy of different signals as a strategy, a relatively short 3/13 (ratio 0.231) combination can be used. I prefer to use the three-way combination 5, 13, 34 (ratios 0.384, 0.147, 0.382) for cluster confirmations.

Rate of Change (ROC) or Momentum

I will not argue with standard wisdom that moving averages perform relatively poorly when markets trend sideways, and that sideways markets occur often. Using moving averages in sideways markets can produce the rapid entries and exits, known as whipsaws, which can be cumulatively quite expensive. The solution to this fault is to stay out of sideways markets, but this could mean many lost opportunities, because one doesn't know the future trend.

Another solution to whipsaws is to seek a confirmation signal before obeying a moving-average entry signal. The confirmation signal should be technically different from the sum of prices which forms the basis of moving averages. My choice is a *rate of change* (*ROC*) *indicator* which measures the rate at which the price is changing compared to a past price.

The accepted standard ROC indicator is actually a ratio of today's price compared with a previous day's price, multiplied by 100.

$$\text{ROC} = \frac{P}{P_n \times 100}$$

where P = today's closing price
P_n = closing price n days ago

Another rate of change indicator, normally called a *momentum indicator,* actually measures the difference in price, converted to a percentage change.

$$\text{MOM} = \frac{(P - P_n) \times 100}{P_n}$$

My preferred ROC indicator, which I call FIRMROC, is approximately an annualized percentage of the difference between today's price and that of 55 days ago.

$$\text{FIRMROC} = \frac{(P - P_{55})}{P_{55}} \times 100 \times \frac{365}{91}$$

I have been asked many times in my seminars why the formula is based on 55 days. I can only reply that 55 days represents the longest time period which I recognize as relevant to today's price and which is also a Fibonacci number. Fifty-five trading days is approximately eleven trading weeks, which is close to a calendar quarter. My final reply is that use of the FIRMROC indicator has worked for me. I encourage readers to experiment with their own indicators. Two suggested formulas to try are shown below. The first is a more mathematically correct annualized percentage ROC representing a 255-trading-day year:

$$\text{55-ROC} = \frac{(P - P_{55})}{P_{55}} \times 100 \times \frac{255}{55}$$

Second, a shorter ROC of 34 days might work in more volatile markets:

$$\text{34-ROC} = \frac{(P - P_{34})}{P_{34}} \times 100 \times \frac{255}{34}$$

The key point about the FIRMROC signal is that, when positive, the market is advancing, when negative, declining, from the point

55 days ago. Zero indicates the market is unchanged. Of most importance to me is the trend of FIRMROC because this indicates to me the conservative momentum of the market. The actual value of FIRMROC is also important when it is at extremely high levels.

In practice, I gauge the trend of FIRMROC by operating my proprietary moving-average software over the data, which is entered into the computer as a file separate to price. This tells me when the FIRMROC trend has changed to provide leading/lagging confirmation of the moving averages on price. Unfortunately my software is not yet publicly available.

The numbers in FIRMROC are too volatile for simple moving averages to work, but another form of moving-average calculation, *moving-average convergence and divergence* (MACD), can and does provide an excellent confirmation indicator at the crossover point.

It should be noted that confirmation of moving-average signals by an indicator such as FIRMROC might be unnecessary where the day-to-day volatility of the market is low. I measure day-to-day volatility by calculating the average daily movement close-to-close (positive or negative makes no difference) as a percentage of the average price over the same time period. The period which I use is the longest moving-average period, but once again I suggest your own experimentation.

If you are using a 3/13 combination, you (or your computer) would calculate the sum of 13-day gains/losses, close-to-close, without regard to positive/negative values. Divide the sum by 13. Divide this average daily movement by the 13-day average closing price. Multiply by 100 to give percentage.

It has been my observation that there is little need for FIRMROC confirmation of moving-average signals where the daily volatility (by my method) is less than 0.5%. Conversely, the FIRMROC confirmation is extremely important where the average daily movement is above 2% of the average price.

I should also mention that the FIRMROC signal becomes unreliable for some time following a major one-day movement in price, such as in a takeover or currency devaluation. The FIRMROC trend often is able to detect insider trading ahead of a takeover or devaluation, but once that event has occurred the huge relative price move renders FIRMROC useless for at least 55 days.

When FIRMROC numbers progress to extremes, the greed or fear of the market is also at extremes. At this time the trader will use very close monitoring techniques to minimize the effect of reversal of trend. In Graph 3-11 the actions of the cotton market in 1995 squeeze conditions are reflected in the top panel (Graph 3-11(*a*)) by a 3/13 moving average of the daily price. The bottom panel shows the MACD of FIRMROC. The FIRMROC reached an extreme of 125 (approximately represents a 125% annual rate of change) at A, at which time risk would have needed to be closely monitored. The moving-average crossover buy at B was confirmed a few days later with the FIRMROC crossover at C. All positions would then have been quit at the moving-average crossover D.

Moving-Average Convergence and Divergence (MACD)

The moving-average convergence and divergence (MACD) indicator was formulated by Gerald Appel in the late 1970s and has since been incorporated in most technical analysis software systems such as Metastock and Tradestation. It was initially conceived to determine overbought and oversold conditions in the stock market, but can be used as a leading indicator to simple moving-average signals.

The MACD reading is the difference between two front-weighted or exponential moving averages. The standard parameters in technical analysis software are 12- and 26-period exponential moving averages. As a rule the shorter-term moving average follows the market more closely than the longer-term moving average. In rising markets the shorter-term moving average trends faster and thus gaps higher than the longer-term average. The MACD measures this gap.

A second signal is provided by the *Signal line,* which, as a standard parameter, is a 9-period exponential moving average of the MACD.

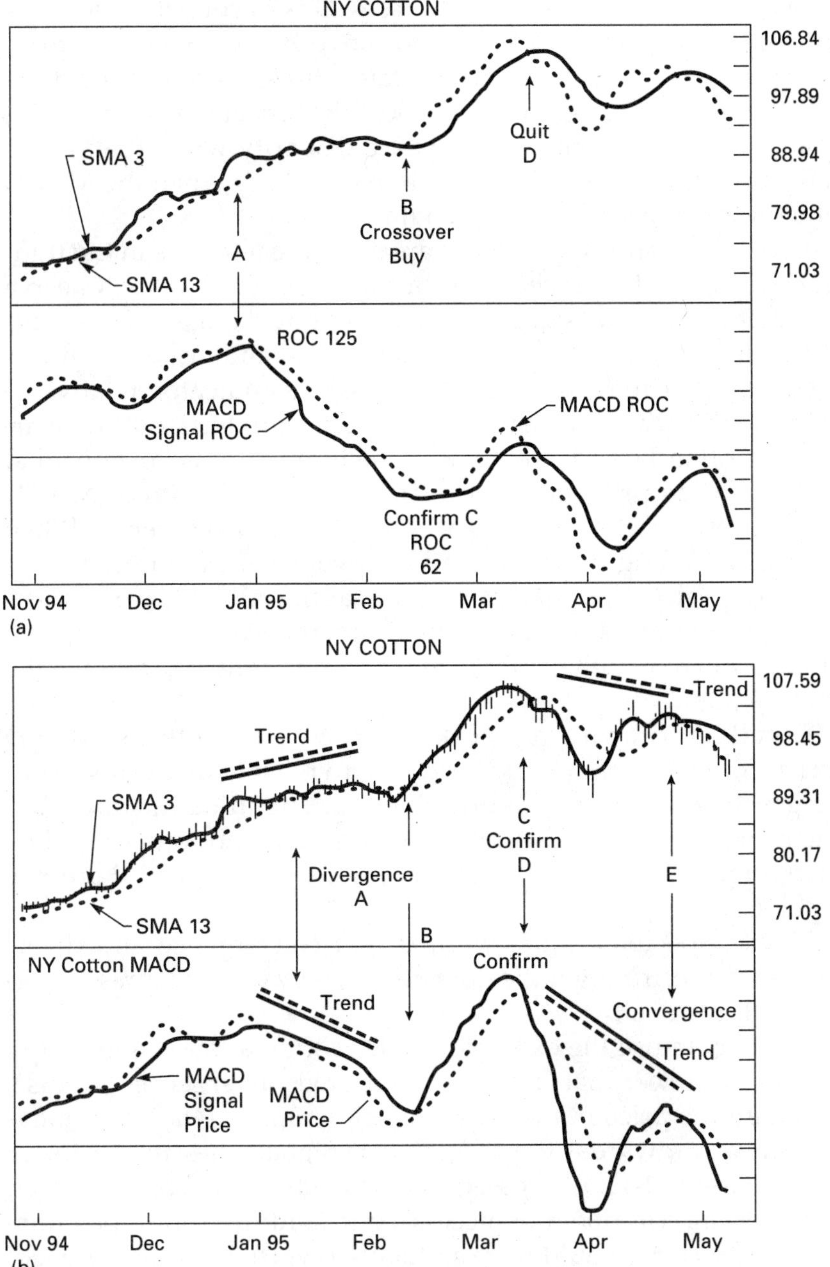

Graph 3-11. Confirmation from New York cotton MACD indicators.

The standard method of using MACD is to confirm price tops or bottoms. If the MACD fails to move higher when the price keeps moving higher, this indicates divergence, particularly when the MACD crosses down below the Signal line. Conversely, at market bottoms, there is negative disparity when the MACD fails to follow the price down, and particularly when the MACD line turns up through the Signal line.

Divergence and convergence are not critical factors in the trading strategies of later chapters, but like any good sailor, I keep a weather eye out for signs that trends might change to my disadvantage. Price, which, as the source of profit and loss, is the major factor in charting, can often be a lagging indicator relative to more sophisticated measures. The underlying thrust of the market can often be judged from momentum or other exponential factors. When price hits a new high, but momentum or MACD fails to also reach a new high, this indicates divergence. When normally leading indicators fail to advance at the same pace as price, or peak earlier than price, then caution should be observed. If other indicators are borderline, divergence might suggest a slight reduction in the number of trades normally indicated in the trading plan.

Trendlines drawn from peaks or troughs on both the MACD and price charts of a market are a more reliable measure of convergence or divergence. If price highs are trending upwards, but the peaks of the MACD plot are in a downtrend, one should be alert for price falls. The subsequent price sell signal could presage a power fall.

Novice speculators are warned that convergence and divergence are confirming indicators. Alone, they do not represent signals to buy or sell.

If we again use the example of 1995 cotton as shown in Graph 3-11(*b*), we see that Point A indicated divergence because, although the price in the upper panel (Graph 3-11(*a*)) kept moving slowly upwards, the MACD and Signal lines in the lower panel (Graph 3-11(*b*)) crossed and moved lower. This indicated that extreme caution was necessary if holding a long position, because the price could have suddenly reversed. As it happened, the price moved higher and was quickly confirmed (convergence) with the MACD/Signal crossover, indicating that fresh long positions could be taken. The market peak C was quickly confirmed by the MACD peak D, suggesting that long positions might be quit. The price and MACD secondary peaks (E) indicate a convergence of an intermediate bear trend.

It should be noted that the MACD calculations can be applied not only to price, but to other indicators. MACD is particularly good at smoothing a volatile series such as FIRMROC. In the strategies that I shall introduce in following chapters, I suggest that the crossover of the MACD and Signal of FIRMROC data is a key signal to trading success.

Gerald Appel has a videotape available (through Signalert Corp.), *The Advanced Moving Average Convergence-Divergence Trading Method.*

Cycles

Psychological Analysis

Earlier in this chapter I touched on crowd psychology, which I believe is the fundamental factor that technical analysis monitors. The direction of commodities and financial markets is determined by thousands of people worldwide—by dealers and computer cowboys, conservative bankers and aggressive fund managers, as well as individual investors, risk managers, and corporate treasurers. Then there are the millions of consumers whose preferences the market participants try to predetermine. Together they make up a crowd. It is the behavior of the crowd which determines the main thrust of the markets. It is my opinion that technical analysis is a method which uses past evidence of crowd behavior, in the form of price patterns, to determine the future actions of the crowd, and thus the market.

Technical analysis could not be successful if price patterns of markets occurred randomly, and from my observations of over thirty years, I can assure readers that although technical analysis is not an exact science, it does provide many important correct forecasts. Technical analysis is only in the 1990s being established as an academic discipline with university chairs commenced in Virginia and California. Next century we might see academics study crowd psychology as part of technical analysis, which in

> *Whoever be the individuals that compose a psychological crowd, however like or unlike be their mode of life, their occupations, their character, or their intelligence, the fact that they have been transformed into a crowd puts them in possession of a sort of collective mind, which makes them feel, think and act in a manner quite different from that in which each individual of them would feel, think, and act were he in a state of isolation. There are certain ideas and feelings which do not come into being, or do not transform themselves into acts except in the case of individuals forming a crowd.*
>
> GUSTAVE LE BON, 1841–1931
> *Psychologie des foules*
> *(translated as The Crowd)*

Box 3-12.

turn might cause economists to venture from mathematical models based on physics.

Business Cycles

One area of technical analysis which is recognized by economists is the existence of periodic business cycles. The classical explanation for the existence of business cycles is that they are a function of modern capitalism caused by the ebb and flow of prosperity and depression which are stimulated by technological change and monetary flow.

The business cycle can be drawn schematically as a sine curve, as explained long ago by Joseph Schumpeter (*Business Cycles*, 1939, reprinted by Porcupine Press, 1982). I have used Schumpeter's illustration of three cycles in Graph 3-12 to show how three symmetrical sine waves could be combined to form the asymmetrical line 4. The economic cycles are a 56-year Kondratieff cycle (curve 1) the 9-year Juglar cycle (curve 2), and the 40-month Kitchin cycle (curve 3), which can be mathematically combined to form line 4.

I have placed a great deal of emphasis on long-term business cycles in forecasting the future economic climate, but such forecasts are for investors and corporate planners, not for market

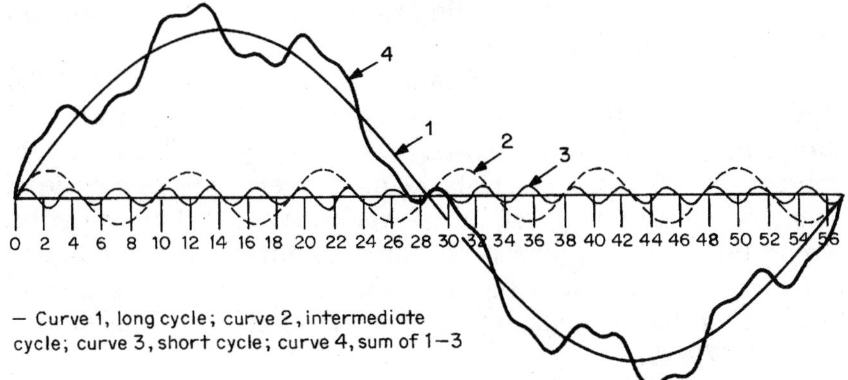

Graph 3-12. Long cycles simulation—sine curve (*courtesy Joseph Schumpeter*, Business Cycles).

traders. In the economic scheme of things, the 40-month Kitchin cycle is fairly short, but it is gigantically long to the trader with a time frame focus of days and hours. A trader needs to look for guidance to short-term cycles of weeks and days which owe more to crowd psychology and seasonal factors than other causes.

Market Cycles

The founder of the Foundation for the Study of Cycles, Edward R. Dewey, recognized that certain activities of people, viewed en masse, fall into definite patterns, some of which repeat themselves with periodic rhythm. Dewey's studies have been confirmed by modern market technicians, of whom Jacob Bernstein must be considered one of the leaders. Serious traders should read at least one of Bernstein's many books for a thorough explanation of cycles.

My own method of using cycles in trading involves a relatively simplistic approach of measuring troughs and peaks of the graphs produced by the MACD on price data (sometimes FIRM-ROC data). Rather than measuring the length of a cycle as the time between peaks or the time between troughs, I measure the period between trough and peak. Also, because as a trader I am intent on recognizing change quickly, I recognize minor peaks and troughs, rather than waiting for the hindsight confirmation of major peaks and troughs.

In the upper panel (*a*) of Graph 3-13, the weekly chart of the Dow Jones Industrial Average in the period June 1990–April 1995 produced cycle troughs of 61, 44, 77, and 33 weeks. This relatively short period, 5 years, suggests a simple-average trough cycle of 53.8 weeks and peak cycle of 57 weeks. A much longer period would be used for practical forecasting, but on this illustrative data a prediction could be made that the next peak is due 57 weeks after the last peak, or within a 6-week period either side of October 27, 1995.

In Graph 3-13(*b*), the same DJIA data is graphed with the MACD indicator. The simple measurement of cycles indicates a possible 53.5-week trough cycle and 61.7-week peak cycle. A simplistic forecast would be for the next MACD peak to occur within a 6-week period either side of January 12, 1996.

My own method of counting wave lengths is illustrated in Graph 3-13(*c*), where the time periods from trough to peak, and peak to trough, are displayed.

An average wave length can be calculated simply as in the previous examples by dividing the sum of weeks by the number of waves, or 25.4 weeks. Because two waves are necessary to make a cycle, the double average of 50.8 weeks is not inconsistent with the cycles as measured in the upper panels (Graph 3-13(*a*) and (*b*)).

My observations over a number of years in a number of markets have suggested to me that waves occur in multiples, and that, therefore, a better average could be achieved if the wave was calculated as a standard wave, or a double wave, or a half wave or a quarter wave. To some degree this is consistent with Elliot Wave theory, which suggests that cycles and/or waves are of different duration. Thus in Graph 3-13(*c*) I can count a 14-week wave as a half wave, the 65-week wave as a double wave, and a 6-week wave as a quarter wave. This changes the calculations so that the sum is divided by 8.25 instead of the simple wave count, 9. The average wave length now becomes 27.8 weeks. Once again, on a relatively short data period, the double-wave average of 55.5 weeks is relatively consistent with previous methods. A simplistic forecast using my method of an average 27.8-week wave from

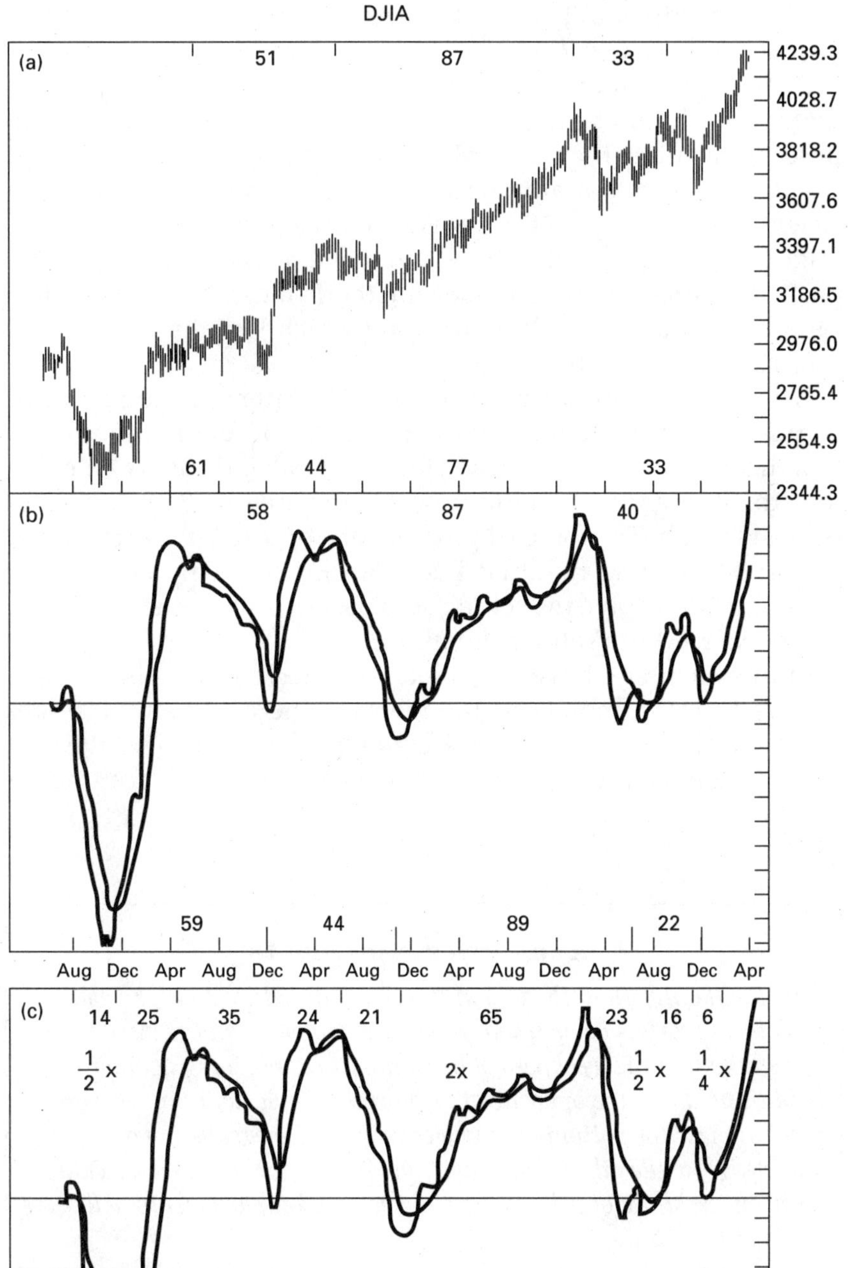

Graph 3-13. MACD peaks and troughs produce cycles.

the last trough would suggest a MACD peak 3 weeks either side of June 30, 1995.

By the time you read this book, the correct date of the intermediate peak should be apparent. I suggest that you use your computer to calculate the weekly MACD of the DJIA.

It can be seen that although the cycles were of generally consistent length, the actual forecasts are disparate. As an analyst I might use a number of methods to make forecasts, and will pay particular attention where those methods indicate a similar date for a peak and trough. It is that date which I might suggest as a forecast peak or trough.

As a trader, I do not wish to pay close attention to forecasts, because profits are made in the present. As a trader I use forecasts to indicate heightened risk. My forecast peak indicates to me that the crowd might be looking to sell in the area 25–31 weeks after the last trough. The forecast peak is not a time to be overextended and to be carrying risk that I can't afford. As a trader I will let other indicators give me selling signals, but my forecast peak tells me to expect those selling signals.

In this chapter I have provided some technical tools to allow traders to make money in the market. The experienced reader will already have much of the knowledge, but I hope that the new wrinkles I have provided will allow some fine tuning of trading

Study Price Movements

If you will only study the weakness of human nature and see what fools these mortals be, you will find it easy to make profits by understanding the weakness of human nature and going against the public and doing the opposite of what other people do. In other words you buy near the bottom on knowledge and sell near the top on knowledge, while other people who just guess, do the opposite. Time spent in the study of price, time and past market movements, will give you a rich reward.

W. D. GANN, 1878–1955

Box 3-13.

systems by veterans. The novice trader will need to study specialized books on technical analysis if he or she wishes to learn more than the rudiments that I have provided. I do believe that the basics covered will allow for a grasp of the tools needed for the following technical strategy.

I have observed and spoken to many market technicians with vast experience and knowledge of sophisticated forms of technical analysis. With a number of notable exceptions, these technicians have not personally been consistently successful traders, because knowledge in itself does not achieve success. Far more important is the strategy to utilize the knowledge to best advantage. This is the key to being a successful trader, and was the key to being a successful privateer.

4

Conservative Strategy: The Plans of a Successful Privateer

Woodes Rogers—Successful Privateer

I mentioned earlier that it is important to differentiate between policy, strategy, and tactics. In my opinion, policy has a time frame of three to five years, and gives general guidance for speculative operations. By now you should have given thought to your own policy or privateer's commission. You also know which technical market tools that I prefer to use, and which can help you reach your goals.

Your next step as a successful speculator is to formulate a strategy which you can comfortably implement. In ancient Greece the word *strategia* meant the art of being a general. The Roman historian Pliny the Elder defined military *strategy* as generalship. In my metaphor of maritime warfare, this means that strategy is the privateer's method of attacking treasure ships, and securing a valuable prize, with least risk to his own ship and crew.

In terms of speculative markets, strategy is the method which indicates which markets to attack, and the time when an attack is likely to be most successful. In later chapters I shall demonstrate tactics, which are the implementation of strategy.

Here let me first tell you a story about a relatively successful privateer. Prior to 1708 the English Crown was entitled to one-tenth of the value of any prize sold by a privateer. In 1708 an Act of Parliament was passed giving the owners and crew of a privateer the whole of the plunder, which no doubt was the incentive behind the formation of a Bristol syndicate to fit out the privateers *Duke* and *Dutchess.* The syndicate chose a young Bristol seaman named Woodes Rogers as leader of the expedition. Although Rogers was not a seasoned commander, he also had no experience as a pirate, and was judged a good leader of men and likely to follow his commission.

The *Duke* and *Dutchess* sailed from Bristol on August 1, 1708, and it was not long before Rogers' command of men was put to the test. Well out to sea, the Captain informed the crews that their destination was the South Seas in a voyage which would last two or three years. While the crews were digesting this unusual information, a merchant vessel was pursued and forced to heave to. Woodes Rogers found that the ship was a neutral Swedish merchant outside his commission, so allowed it to proceed without any confiscation of cargo.

The men protested strongly in a mutinous outburst. Rogers immediately clapped ten seamen in irons and had the ringleader lashed with a knotted rope. He explained to the rest of the crew why the Swedish vessel was outside the privateering commission. Happily for Rogers, the capture of a small Spanish barque soon satisfied the larcenous nature of the crew and the voyage south continued without incident.

Although inexperienced in waters distant from England, Rogers had the guidance of a pilot—the ex-buccaneer Captain William Dampier, who had previously circumnavigated the world in the *Roebuck.* By April 1709, operating off the west coast of South America, Rogers had captured four ships, but he was

Robinson Crusoe

In January 1709 the *Duke* rescued a marooned sailor named Alexander Selkirk, who had been stranded on an island by his pirate captain, alone for over four years. Many years later Daniel Defoe was to read Rogers' and Dampier's accounts of Selkirk's adventure, and produce a fictionalized tale entitled *The Life and Strange Surprising Adventures of Robinson Crusoe of York, Mariner.* Defoe's storytelling powers have kept Robinson Crusoe alive for two centuries, but the names of those with a hand in the original story have faded into obscurity.

Box 4-1.

running short of water. The council of officers decided that if they must land on the Spanish-dominated continent they might as well launch an attack. The lightly defended Peruvian port of Guayaquil was attacked and held to ransom.

The great prize which Rogers sought was the Manila Galleon. Once or twice a year the Spanish loaded a huge vessel with spices, porcelain, gold, and exquisite artifacts for a voyage from the Philippine garrison in Manila to the Mexican port of Acapulco. This huge galleon, called *Nao de Chine* by the Spanish, could be called the richest prize in the world and was no doubt the main target of Rogers' voyage.

Rogers prepared to ambush the Manila Galleon by ransoming two of his prize ships and converting another to a fighting ship with the name next in line of the peerage, *Marquis.* Rogers' small fleet of three vessels sailed a pattern over the course that the galleon should have to take. They had a long wait because the galleon was in fact two months overdue.

Water and provisions were desperately low when a sail appeared. Two of the fleet attacked, and Rogers was wounded in the short battle in which the *Duke* forced the enemy to strike its colors. The prize was not the great galleon but a lesser treasure ship *Incarnacion,* which had left Manila with the main vessel *Begona,* but had become separated from it.

Two days later the great Manila Galleon was sighted. Rogers' intelligence reports had not prepared him for the size and heavy arms of the prize. The *Begona* was a huge vessel, planked with tough wood from the Philippines which the largest cannonballs could not pierce. Her twelve-pound cannon far outweighed the six-pounders of the *Duke, Dutchess,* and *Marquis.* False decks four stories high made boarding nearly impossible, even if the contingent of soldiers could be overcome. Nevertheless the three privateer fighting ships valiantly attacked the treasure ship.

Rogers was wounded again when the *Duke's* mainmast shattered. With the *Dutchess'* rigging in tatters, it was an obvious decision to withdraw and allow the Manila Galleon to lumber on toward Mexico. Rogers was later to write that any further damage to his vessels might have emboldened the Spanish to turn attacker, which would have placed the earlier prizes at risk. Rogers' main prize was allowed to escape. Once the ships were repaired, the privateer fleet commenced its long journey through the Pacific and Indian Oceans back to England, eventually arriving in October 1711.

The privateering voyage was successful even if it did miss the main prize. Rogers' command had circumnavigated the world with its original ships, with losses of only fifty men, performed to its commission, and returned with rewards. Why was a young and untried Bristol sea captain successful in a privateering voyage when many men in the sixteenth and seventeenth centuries failed?

First, he held rigidly to his commission, which was to pursue, attack, and seize enemy ships in the South Sea. The enemy was France, allied to Spain.

Second, Rogers was provided with sufficient resources for the quest. The owners had countered the threat of mutiny by doubling the usual complement of officers under a written constitution. An officers' committee on each ship, and joint council for both the *Duke* and *Dutchess,* were to be in agreement on all major matters.

Rogers had strong intelligence about his major target from the ex-buccaneer Captain William Dampier—the "Pilot for the South Sea." Dampier had preserved his charts and journals from previous adventures, rolled up in lengths of bamboo sealed with wax.

Most important, Rogers had the ability to command. He was equally able to sway the officers' council as an at times mutinous and sickened crew. When his efforts to persuade were insufficient, he knew when to compromise to achieve a reasonable result. He focused on the major prize with great patience, but knew when to cut his losses and withdraw.

Formulation of a Technical Strategy for Speculation

What does the story of an eighteenth-century privateer have to do with speculation in the stock and futures markets? As I told you at the beginning of the book, I believe that lessons of the past can be used as guidance for the future. Although technology is much changed since Rogers' day, the emotions of human beings in search of treasure are basically the same. By using elements of Rogers' strategy on his privateer voyage, I have formulated a speculative strategy which has proved extremely profitable in futures markets, and will provide you with the framework to successfully trade the markets chosen by your policy. (See Box 4-2 for sample results of this system.)

Most of my trading life in commodities and finance has been concerned with defending the wealth of others, by trading one or two markets for the sole purpose of risk management. I used a variety of techniques to trade those few markets with overall success, but with some notably bad setbacks. One German client made good speculative money trading *opposite* my risk management recommendations for 6 months, before he gave it all back when my techniques resumed working.

In financial risk management one does not have a choice of markets. One must do one's best to make hedge recommendations, even when conditions are erratic. In speculation one has the luxury of choosing the markets in which to trade, and the time of entry and exit. If a market is trading erratically, it is prudent not to trade that market.

I have designed a strategy which chooses which markets to trade only at times when the chances of success are high. If my

1993 Flash Results

Period: February 5, 1993–November 30, 1993

Completed trades	61
Profitable trades	36
Losing trades	25
Profit/loss trade ratio	1.44:1
Dollar profits	$1,684,920
Dollar losses	$248,768
Net dollar profit	$1,436,156
Average profit per trade	$46,803
Average loss per trade	$9,951
Dollar per trade profit/loss ratio	**4.704:1**
Average profit per trade excluding three largest profits	$30,516
Dollar per trade profit/loss ratio excluding three largest profits	3.067:1
Maximum drawdown	$81,510 (6.5% capital)
Maximum loss	$34,800 (2.8% capital)
Maximum profit	$251,016 (30.6% capital)
Return on capital	**1436.15%**

Box 4-2.

speculative activity was confined to only one or two markets, this strategy would mean long periods of time out of the markets. The oil and gold markets, once beautiful markets to trade, have not produced opportunities for my system for some years before 1995.

Being out of a market is a quite comfortable state for my personality. Many speculators are not comfortable with long periods of trading inactivity. I have already mentioned the need for discipline in a trader's attitude. It takes at least as much discipline not to trade as it does to implement the right decisions when trading.

Think about it. The successful privateer or pirate did not fight all the time. There were long periods of waiting between those exciting sword fights. Constant battle normally means incurring many painful injuries, which at least debilitate, and at most cause death.

My strategy overcomes the long periods of waiting by monitoring up to fifty international markets by computer. It is as if the privateer searching for treasure could track fifty ships using a spy satellite and attack only those which promise great success. It would be extremely difficult to obtain quality intelligence to allow fundamental analysis of such a large number of markets, so the basis of the strategy needs to be technical. Computerized technical analysis can track a huge number of markets, providing the program knows what it is looking for.

This does not mean that I do not use fundamental analysis in my trading. When I identify a market opportunity, I also examine the fundamentals because I like the fundamental and technical analysis to agree. When they disagree, I might still proceed, but with caution. At many times I have noted that markets' technical signals occur in advance of what fundamentals dictate. In some markets this is due to insider trading.

In 1991 I noticed that the deutsche mark was weakening technically without any apparent fundamental cause. Someone was selling marks and buying dollars. The strategy of the mark seller became apparent only a few days later on August 19, when the world learned of the leadership coup in Russia. The dollar rose against the mark from USD/DEM 1.7212 on August 15 to 1.8340 on August 19. I have learned to trust my technical analysis.

The technique which forms the basis of my strategy is *trend following,* which means that I am guided by what the market has done, and is doing, rather than forecasting what the market might do. The only forecast that a trend-following system makes is that the current trend is likely to continue for sufficient time to allow profitable entry and exit.

I have read many comments by professional traders indicating suspicion of trend-following methods and stressing their opinion that much of the time markets do not trend. These comments have increased in frequency with the expansion of technology which allows markets to be followed on computer screens tick by tick. Many professionals have to follow these tick movements, and sometimes lose sight of the larger picture. When a market is viewed over time frames of days, weeks, and months, the general trending nature becomes self-evident.

The difficulty that many market professionals have with trend following is that prudence dictates periods of inactivity, which clashes with a psychological need to constantly trade. These people must, and do, use different techniques to satisfy their needs (and sometimes those of their employer), and of course many are successful. This does not mean that trend following is an inept technique. It means that the policy of many professionals does not allow them to use a trend-following strategy.

During the thirty years in which I have been monitoring and trading markets, I have been fortunate to experience a number of major booms and busts in foreign exchange, wool, cattle, gold, silver, stocks, and bonds. I can assure readers that the big gains which allow speculators to make fortunes occur in trends.

The unique feature of the trading system which I am about to demonstrate is that it eliminates many of the small losses which critics of trend following hate about the method. The strategy is designed to produce large profits from strong surges and collapses, while limiting entry to markets which might produce a series of small losses.

There are five main components in this system, which chooses the most opportune time to trade in which market:

1. Moving averages—daily, weekly, monthly
2. MACD—daily, weekly, monthly
3. Rate of change—daily, weekly, monthly
4. Synergy of three indicators over time frames—daily, weekly, monthly
5. Weekly cycles as measured by MACD

The technical details of moving averages, MACD, rate of change, and cycles were all covered in Chapter 3. In the Woodes Rogers strategy, I simply provide a method of combining these trend-following methods so as to provide synergistic low-risk/high-reward trading opportunities.

The Woodes Rogers Speculative Strategy

My reconstruction of the privateer Woodes Rogers' strategy suggests that he identified the Manila Galleon as his main prize; patiently moved to intercept the approximate course of the main prize, while capturing other prizes of opportunity; and attacked. When the main attack failed, Rogers withdrew quickly in order to secure previous gains.

My strategy for speculation in stocks and futures markets has similar elements to Woodes Rogers'. The system seeks to identify markets which have commenced the large trend moves which produce large profits; the course of the trend is calculated to suggest an entry point; the entry can be fine-tuned to tactical excellence. An exit point is calculated daily to provide controlled-risk exit if necessary, but otherwise the trader will stay in the market until a change of trend is indicated.

Moving Averages

In my privateer analogy, the moving average can be likened to the wake of a sailing vessel—it defines the course that the ship has taken and is taking. The helmsman is constantly turning the wheel to make minor adjustments to stay on a set course against the influences of the wind and current. These minor turns are lost in the smooth wake. A large sailing vessel cannot reverse. It can change direction relatively slowly, with the wake producing a curved signal that it is doing so.

In Chapter 3 on technical analysis, I indicated how the moving average smooths out the daily fluctuations, like a sailing vessel's wake. The basic premise of trend following is that no market can stage a sustained uptrend unless buying pressure is constantly stronger than selling pressure. Conversely a meaningful downtrend can occur only when selling pressure predominates. A moving average will indicate the current balance between buying pressure and selling pressure.

I have also illustrated (see Graph 3-9) how a moving average of a short time span will indicate the change of buying/selling pressure in that time frame, compared to a moving average of a longer time span. When two moving averages cross, the crossover point can be taken as a buying or selling signal.

I learned long ago that the selection of the time spans of the simple moving average was critical to the success of a trend-following system. In the 1960s, when trading wool and wool futures, I enjoyed success in managing risk from a combination of a 10-day moving average and a 50-day moving average. Wool in those days was a relatively slow-moving commodity traded in a gentlemanly fashion by established wool merchants and mills. In the late 1960s the Russians became a new market force, at a time when the supply/demand picture was fragile. The result was a fast-moving boom and bust market in which my 10/50-day simple moving averages were far too slow in giving meaningful signals. I quickly switched to a 5-day and 20-day moving-average combination, which enabled resumption of a successful trading pattern.

I subsequently discovered that one of the world's most consistent trading funds was started by U.S. broker Richard Donchian in 1961 based on a combination of 5- and 20-day moving averages, modified by volatility penetration criteria. Donchian personalized his system by adding many judgmental factors relating to the extent to which the 20-day average must be penetrated and the day of the week the signal occurred. Many readers might be familiar with the Wall Street success of Elaine Gazarelli, who was an early disciple of Donchian.

I had much success trading interest rate futures using the Fibonacci sequence combination 5-day and 21-day simple moving averages, and taught many bank treasury traders this method in the late 1970s. I recently discovered that one of my early pupils, now a bank treasurer, still uses the 5/21-day combination to assess independently the recommendations from his staff who use "rocket scientist" techniques.

My personal approach to moving averages was to develop a computer program which optimizes the correct combination of moving averages on any given day. This program forms the basis of "black box" risk management software which will be marketed when there is more widespread acceptance of structured risk management—i.e., when the current frequent trading management culture fades. This flexible moving-average program is also the signal producer for my highly successful FLASH speculative system (Box 4-2), but this is not currently available to you for your system.

Through trial and error I have formulated the combination of 3-day and 13-day moving averages as the driving force of the Woodes Rogers Speculative Strategy, instead of my own "black box" system. Used on its own, the 3/13-day moving-average combination will produce a large number of small losing trades in most markets, and a few reasonably profitable trades. To avoid many unsuccessful trades, I have introduced two important changes to the normal actions by moving-average traders.

The first important rule is that positions are not reversed when the two moving averages cross over. Some moving-average traders buy when the 3-period average crosses above the 13-period average, then sell back and go short simultaneously when the short average crosses down below the long average. The Woodes Rogers strategy dictates that *a position is taken only when the daily moving average crosses in the direction of the market indicated by the rate-of-change* (ROC) *weekly indicator.*

The basis of this rule is my philosophy that a change of direction in the market can signal time to quit positions or leave the market, but only rarely indicates that the new trend will be maintained for sufficient time to immediately profit from it. Reversing positions with moving-average signals means that one is constantly in the market; this goes against our basic strategy of profiting only from major trend moves.

The second important rule for entry is that the moving average is calculated on the period's high or low in the direction which the trend is taking.

When the market is rising, calculate the 3- and 13-period averages from the period highs: Entry is made on the highs' crossover.

When the market is falling, calculate the 3- and 13-period averages from the period lows: Entry is made on the lows' crossover.

Because the 3/13-period combination is relatively short, a volatile market can produce many signals if the moving average is calculated simply on period closes. It must be remembered that an uptrend occurs when a market makes a series of higher highs, and is changed to a downtrend when a series of lower lows commences. A moving average on the *high* illustrates a series of *higher highs.* A moving average on the *low* illustrates a series of *lower lows.* Most computer programs can calculate averages on highs and lows.

The last method that I have introduced to identify significant trading opportunities is the operation of the 3/13-period combination over a series of time frames. The Woodes Rogers strategy calculates 3/13-period combinations on *daily data, weekly data,* and *monthly data.*

Many traders ignore the longer time frames because they believe that they are not relevant in day-to-day actions. I have found that it is in the longer time frames that crowd psychology has its strongest influence. It is the cumulative effect of large-trader activity over days, weeks, and months which establishes the strong moods of the crowds that ensure continuation of a trend for a period of months. Except in times of crisis, it takes highly significant daily activity for a number of days to change the mood of the crowd.

The optimum trade will occur when the daily, weekly, and monthly trends are moving in concert. In the system which you will operate, this means that the last crossover signals of the 3/13 moving-average combination will have given buy signals on daily, weekly, and monthly data or sell signals on daily, weekly, and monthly data. When all signals are in accord, the chances of success are high.

In practice, we cannot always wait for the optimum trade and must be prepared to compromise by entering a market at a time when we calculate that the market might be moving toward the optimum.

The Rogers strategy tabulates the position of the last signals for daily, weekly, and monthly time frames onto a worksheet. The signals can be generated by the computer from standard software programs such as Computrac, Metastock, or TradeStation or from spreadsheet calculations. Graph 4-1 shows the 3/13-period combination over the daily, weekly, and monthly charts of IBM.

It can be noted that the monthly chart (Graph 4-1(*c*)) displays an old buy signal (3/13-month moving-average crossover calcu-

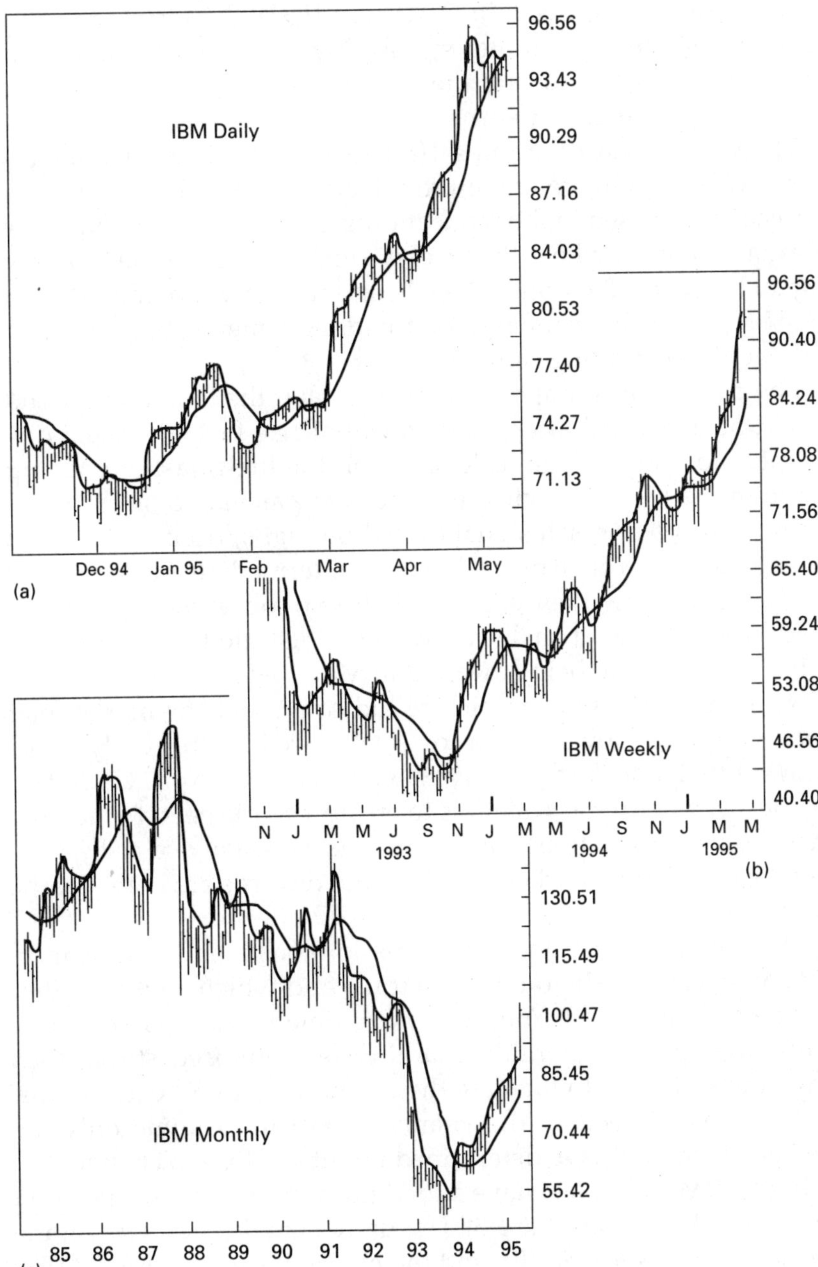

Graph 4-1. IBM daily, weekly, and monthly simple moving averages.

lated on the high crossed in December 1993). Because of the current rising trend the moving averages were calculated on monthly highs to indicate the buy points. Long trend periods exceeding 1 year can be seen.

The weekly chart (Graph 4-1(*b*)) also displays old buy signals 3/13-week moving-average crossovers calculated on the high; the earliest crossed in the week ending October 22, 1993. Note the normal situation where the weekly signal preceded the monthly signal by nearly 2 months. Weekly and monthly moving-average signals are confirmation of long trend movements, but much too slow to use as trading signals.

The daily chart (Graph 4-1(*a*)) shows that the long rising trend might be at an end after an exponential rise in 1995. The 3-day simple moving average (calculated on the high) last crossed up through the 13-day moving average (also calculated on the high) on April 4, 1995. A sell signal (based on highs) occurred 10 days after what might have proved to be an intermediate peak on April 27. Because of the then probable falling trend, moving averages were then calculated on daily lows (not illustrated), but the action sell signal was still being awaited in May 1995.

So the moving-average picture indicated that the market had been trending upwards for over a year, but the daily chart showed that a peak might have been reached on April 27, 1995.

The last step in the system is to create a worksheet. Remember that the strategy is to monitor many markets daily so as to identify the one or two markets in which the rewards are high and the risks low.

The policy (or privateer's commission) has identified the markets or stocks which you wish to trade and which could number as high as a hundred. You don't have time to minutely examine daily, weekly, and monthly charts of one hundred stocks each day. It is sufficient to tabulate the recent position of each indicator on a worksheet. In this manner you can examine only the charts which you have determined might be close to change.

In the IBM example, I have added the moving-average position to the worksheet in Box 4-3. The daily signal is *bought* (B); the weekly signal is *bought* (B); and the monthly signal is *bought* (B).

Now we can examine the next indicator, MACD.

Moving-Average Worksheet
Moving Averages—Daily, Weekly, Monthly Worksheet, May 12, 1995

	Moving-average signal*			MACD signal†			ROC signal‡				
Market	D	W	M	D	W	M	D	W	M	W	M
Weight	2	4	2	1	3	1	1	4	2	20	
IBM	B	B	B								
				Total weight:	/	=	%				

*Moving-average signal: 3/13 combination crossover.
†MACD signal: peak or trough.
‡ROC signal: MACD on FIRMROC crossover.

Box 4-3.

MACD—Moving Average Convergence and Divergence

As explained in Chapter 3 on technical analysis, the MACD consists of a *MACD line,* which is the difference between long and short exponential moving averages (standard 12-26), and a *Signal line,* which is the exponential moving average of the *MACD line.* The MACD line is a leading indicator which tends to peak or trough simultaneously with or very close to the actual price peak or trough, which was illustrated in Graph 3-11.

I mentioned earlier that the moving average showed where the market had been, like the wake of a sailing vessel. This is helpful to the trader, but an early warning signal would be nice, so that we might determine that the course is going to change.

If you were looking at a sailing ship through a telescope, you would be able to note that a change of course might occur, because the helmsman or skipper would order the sails adjusted to make the new course possible. At the time of the change, the sails would be rerigged to gain advantage of the wind. The new course would then become visible in the wake.

This is how I use the MACD indicator in the Woodes Rogers strategy. The MACD gives an early warning of change of direction when the MACD line shows a peak or trough. I use standard MACD computer calculations, which are included in most technical analysis software programs, on the *close.* To some degree, MACD calculations on the close counterbalance the use of moving averages based on highs and lows.

I have found that the daily MACD by its very nature is erratic. The weekly MACD is much more consistent, and I rate its signal highly. The monthly MACD peaks and troughs occur much faster than the moving-average signals, but are still too slow for anything but confirmation of short-time-frame changes of trend. Graph 4-2 shows the *MACD line* and MACD signal of the IBM price data for the period preceding May 12, 1995.

It can be noted on Graph 4-2(*c*) that the last monthly MACD indicator was a *trough* in September 1993 confirmed by the crossover of the MACD line and MACD signal in November 1993.

Graph 4-2(*b*) shows that the last weekly turning point was a *trough* in the week ending February 24, 1995, and was confirmed by the crossover two weeks later.

Graph 4-2(*a*) demonstrates the sharp fall that an exponential indicator like the MACD can take once a *peak* (here reached on April 28, 1995) has occurred.

The peaks and troughs can be identified two periods after they actually occur, and confirmed with the MACD line and MACD Signal crossover.

The last signals for each time frame are then recorded on the worksheet. In the IBM illustration, the daily *peak* (P), the weekly *trough* (T), and monthly *trough* (T) were recorded as per Box 4-4.

As mentioned in Chapter 3, the standard use of MACD is to check convergence or divergence of peaks and troughs with price peaks and troughs. When peaks or troughs converge (occur in similar patterns), the price trend is thought to be confirmed. When the MACD peaks or troughs form a different pattern from the price peaks or troughs, then the price trend might be false. I keep an eye on convergence and divergence but do not consciously include it in my system.

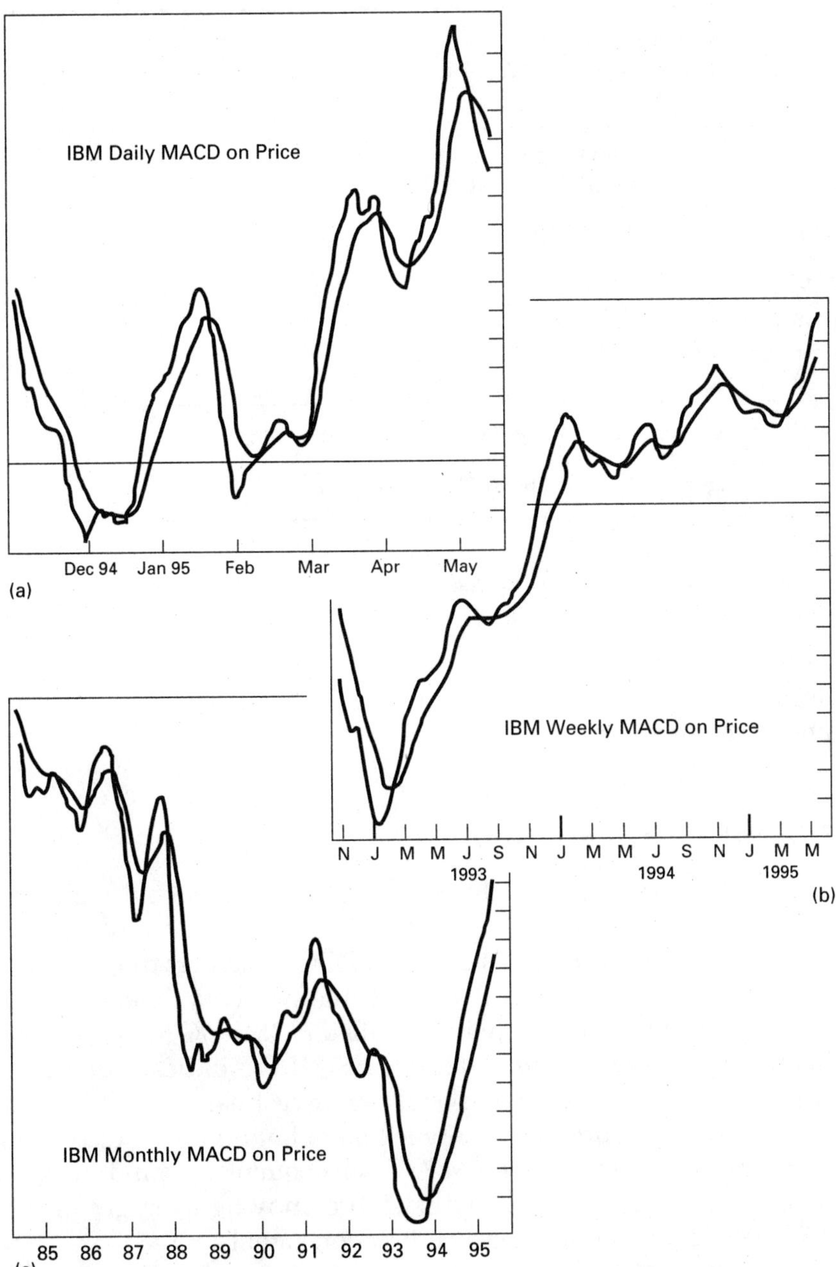

Graph 4-2. IBM daily, weekly, and monthly MACD on price.

MACD Worksheet
MACD on Price—Daily, Weekly, Monthly Worksheet, May 12, 1995

	Moving-average signal*			MACD signal†			ROC signal‡			
Market	D	W	M	D	W	M	D	W	M	W M
Weight	2	4	2	1	3	1	1	4	2	20
IBM				P	T	T				
				Total weight:	/	=	%			

*Moving-average signal: 3/13 combination crossover.
†MACD signal: peak or trough.
‡ROC signal: MACD on FIRMROC crossover.

Box 4-4.

I will return to MACD peaks and troughs again later when I discuss cycles, but now wish to examine the use of MACD on rate-of-change data.

Rate of Change (ROC)

The standard use of rate of change (ROC), also known as "momentum," is to give a guide to the speed of a market's advance or decline. The standard momentum and ROC indicators did not give the percentage change that I was looking for at the time, so I formulated my own indicator, which I called FIRMROC (explained in Chapter 3). I initially formulated the FIRMROC indicator to compare various international markets in an investment model, which has shown a noncumulative, nonleveraged annual rate of return exceeding 20% since 1986–1987. I subsequently found that a change point measured by my black box moving averages or by MACD gave dependable market direction signals.

My daily routine is to key the computer to collect price data from my data provider, and then to run a ROC program. Most technical programs have routines (as do spreadsheets) which can

Calculating FIRMROC

Example: IBM

AGO_{55}	$74^{56}/_{64}$ (price 55 days ago)
Today	$94^{24}/_{64}$ (price today)
Diff	$19^{32}/_{64}$ (difference)

$$\text{FIRMROC} = \frac{\text{DIFF}}{\text{AGO}_{55}} \times \frac{36{,}500}{91}$$

$$= 104.5\% \ (\%\ \text{ROC annualized})$$

Roughly annualized percentage change from 55 days ago

Box 4-5.

be formulated to calculate ROC from the *close* price data. Even though my moving-average indicators are calculated on highs or lows, I keep the balance by calculating the ROC indicator (and the MACD on price) on the close. I enter the ROC data manually into the computer, but there are formulas to make this data entry automatic in some software programs.

Once the FIRMROC data is entered, I use the MACD facility to assess market activity. While I use the MACD facility on price data to determine peaks and troughs, on ROC I am interested only in the crossover point of the MACD line and MACD signal.

The MACD on ROC data cannot be said always to be a leading indicator such as the MACD on price data. The MACD on ROC sometimes leads the moving-average signal, and sometimes lags, depending on the strength of the market.

I have already used the analogies of the moving average as the wake of a sailing vessel, and the MACD on price as the signs of a change of rigging. The ROC can be likened to the direction and strength of the wind which drives the sailing ship. The optimum course for a sailor is to be driven before a strong, steady wind with course and rigging attuned. If the wind is too light, too strong, or from the wrong direction, then the vessel's course can be erratic.

The optimum trade in a trend-following system is a purchase or sale at the start of a trend in which the market moves steadily toward a trading objective. Such optimum trades rarely occur, but we can identify when a market's momentum and leading indicators are in accord with moving averages, so that the chances for success are high.

The strategy monitors the ROC over daily, weekly, and monthly time frames in a similar manner to the other indicators.

In Graph 4-3 it can be noted in panel (*c*) that the monthly ROC indicated a *buy* signal when the MACD line and MACD signal crossed up in November 1993. This time the ROC was a leading indicator, suggesting that August 1993 was indeed a major trough.

Graph 4-3(*b*) also indicates that a *buy* signal has occurred, this time on the crossover in the week ending February 17, 1995.

Graph 4-3(*a*) once again indicates the exponential nature of a fall which can accompany a significant peak. The actual MACD on ROC *sell* signal occurred on May 3, 1995, only four days after the IBM price peak.

Once again the indicators are recorded on the worksheet as in Box 4-6, where the daily time frame shows a *sell* (S).

We have now recorded the key directional signal for the Woodes Rogers strategy. *The weekly MACD on ROC indicates the direction of the intermediate trend. The strategy will seek to trade only in the direction of the weekly ROC indicator.*

In the IBM example that I have been illustrating, the most recent weekly ROC signal was *buy* (Graph 4-3(*b*)). This means that the system is remaining *long* providing the synergy of all the signals indicates that the bull trend continues. The daily signals have indicated an early warning of a correction, but profits will not be taken until the synergy is sufficiently weakened.

Synergy of All Indicators

The problem with monitoring a number of technical indicators is that most people cannot decide which indicator is the key signal at the time. One of the simplest systems that I have encountered

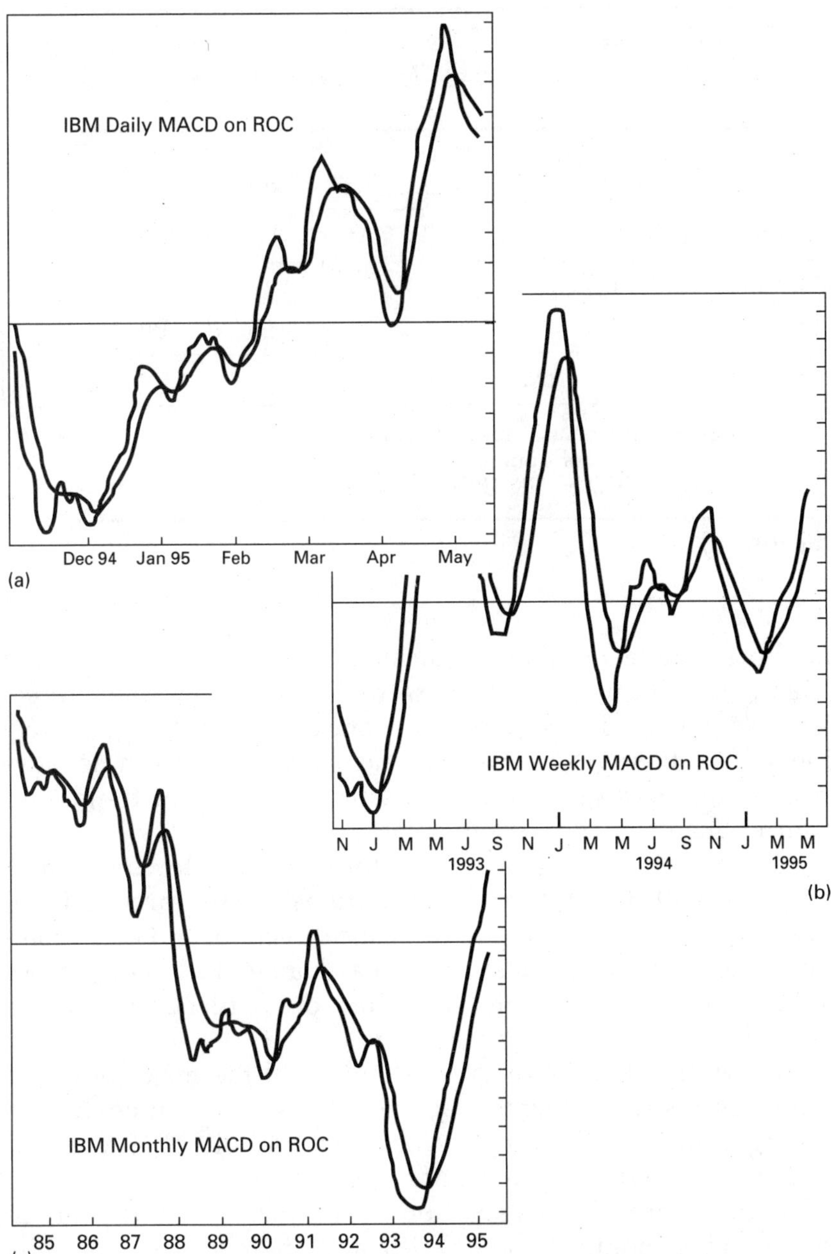

Graph 4-3. IBM daily, weekly, and monthly MACD on ROC.

ROC Worksheet
MACD on ROC—Daily, Weekly, Monthly Worksheet,
May 12, 1995

	Moving-average signal*			MACD signal†			ROC signal‡				
Market	D	W	M	D	W	M	D	W	M	W	M
Weight	2	4	2	1	3	1	1	4	2	20	
IBM							S	B	B		

Total weight: / = %

*Moving-average signal: 3/13 combination crossover.
†MACD signal: peak or trough.
‡ROC signal: MACD on FIRMROC crossover.

Box 4-6.

monitored three oscillator indicators. Trading positions were taken when all three oscillators were pointing in the same direction, and positions were quit if only one oscillator changed direction. In fact, this system was not much better than a simple moving average because it was successful only in long trends but incurred many small losses in volatile markets.

The Woodes Rogers strategy has three trend-following indicators, each with three different time frames. Only rarely will all nine indicators be pointing in the same direction, and often complete agreement occurs just prior to a change of direction. If we waited until this optimum condition, our patience as traders would be stretched to the breaking point.

One solution would be to wait only until the majority of the indicators were signaling the same trend. If six out of nine showed a rising trend, we would buy. When only four out of nine stayed long, we would quit our positions.

The problem with this solution is that three indicators are in slow-moving monthly time frames, and another three are quite volatile daily signals. We would increase trading opportunities without reducing risk.

What I have done is to try to emulate life experience in which we learn that some indicators are more valuable than others. Through trial and error I have placed a numerical value on each indicator, according to my experience. The daily simple moving average was twice as valuable as the MACD on price. The weekly MACD on ROC is considered twice as valuable as the monthly moving average.

The numerical values placed on the individual indicators add up to 20. If all indicators are showing the same trend, the numerical values would add up to 20, or 100% of the total. If only some indicators, totaling a value of 6, showed one direction, then the overall system would be showing a value of 30%.

Synergy of all the indicators is achieved by:

1. Noting the direction of the weekly MACD on ROC signal, which is the direction of the strategy.
2. Adding the numerical values of all indicators in that direction: short, all P's and S's; long, all T's and B's.
3. Dividing the total value by 0.2 to achieve a percentage.
4. Choosing to enter the market only when the percentage is above, say, 65%.

In Box 4-7 the weekly MACD on ROC is *bought* (B). The total of all *bought* indicators (B's and T's) on May 12, 1995, was 2 + 4 + 2 + 3 + 1 + 4 + 2 = 18. A percentage is achieved by dividing the total 18 by 0.2 = 90. The IBM market, as measured by system synergy, is 90% long—or rising with a 90% chance of continuing to rise for sufficient time to make a profit from buying stock, once the daily indicators recover.

This system works quite well, and I stress that the numerical values are from my personal judgment based on my own experience. If you are an experienced stock market trader with a more adventurous spirit, you might well make different value judgments. I suggest again that you can use my system as a template, and adjust according to your own policy and judgment.

My conservative policy led me to make one final adjustment to the synergy by taking into account the length of time that a market had already been trending in the one direction.

Woodes Rogers Weighting
Weighted Signals—Daily, Weekly, Monthly

	Moving-average signal*			MACD signal†			ROC signal‡				
Market	D	W	M	D	W	M	D	W	M	W	M
Weight	2	4	2	1	3	1	1	4	2		20
IBM	B	B	B	P	T	T	S	B	B		18

Total weight: 18/20 = 90% long

*Moving-average signal: 3/13 combination crossover.
†MACD signal: peak or trough.
‡ROC signal: MACD on FIRMROC crossover.

Box 4-7.

Trading Cycles

Cycles were discussed in Chapter 3 and are an important tool in forecasting markets. The Woodes Rogers Strategy is a method for trading, not forecasting. Too many good technical analysts fail in their trading because they cannot separate forecasting from actuality. I found a way to use cycles as a trading tool by modifying my synergy calculations.

First, why worry about cycles in the first place? Because, as my experience has shown, a number of losses from trading trend-following systems occur because the trend is well advanced before the trading position is taken. In other words, by the time all the indicators were pointing in the same direction, hidden market factors were already at work providing a basis for a change of direction.

I will use a sailing analogy again. A sailing vessel can only proceed directly on course to its destination providing the wind is following in the direction of that destination. Most of the time a sailing boat can use only part of the force of the wind coming from a direction other than toward its destination. It sails obliquely backward and forward across the direct course toward its destination. This is known as "tacking."

In a sailing race, or when privateers roamed the oceans, someone observing the sailing vessel could calculate how long the tack in one direction would last simply by knowing the final destination and the direction of the wind.

I used my sailing experience in trading markets by trying to calculate how long a trend would progress before it was likely to change tack. The practical method which I chose would probably horrify cycle experts like Jake Bernstein, but it has provided the success that a practical trader seeks.

In the previous section on MACD on price, I described how I use the peak and trough of the MACD line as a leading indicator. I found that in many markets the MACD on weekly price produced a relatively regular pattern, simulating a cyclical rhythm. By calculating the average length between peak and trough, as well as trough to peak, I could roughly forecast when a trend would end. It was only a rough forecast which had a number of failures, so that I would not recommend its use as a speculator's only analysis tool.

As explained in Chapter 3 (see under "Cycles"), the successful forecasts improved when I divided the peaks and troughs into double and half cycles. For instance, there would be occasions when the trend continued past its average termination point in a strong movement that was approximately double the average length. At other times, a market would have only a short burst which would terminate at approximately half the average time. Rather than consider these aberrations longer or shorter cycles than normal, I called them double cycles or half cycles.

In Graph 4-4 the MACD on the price of the IBM stock at first glance suggests simply a trough in January 1993 and maybe moving toward a peak in mid-1995. There are, however, a number of minor peaks and troughs which I have identified and marked with the number of weeks of duration.

The longest trend, from a July 1992 peak to the January 1993 low, was 27 weeks. This I have labeled as a double-cycle wave. Two short trends of 6 weeks and 9 weeks have been identified as half-cycle waves. One short trend of 4 weeks has been labeled as a quarter cycle.

Without any such labeling the total period of 151 weeks might have been divided by 10 waves to produce an average trend length of 15 weeks. My method of identifying double- and half-

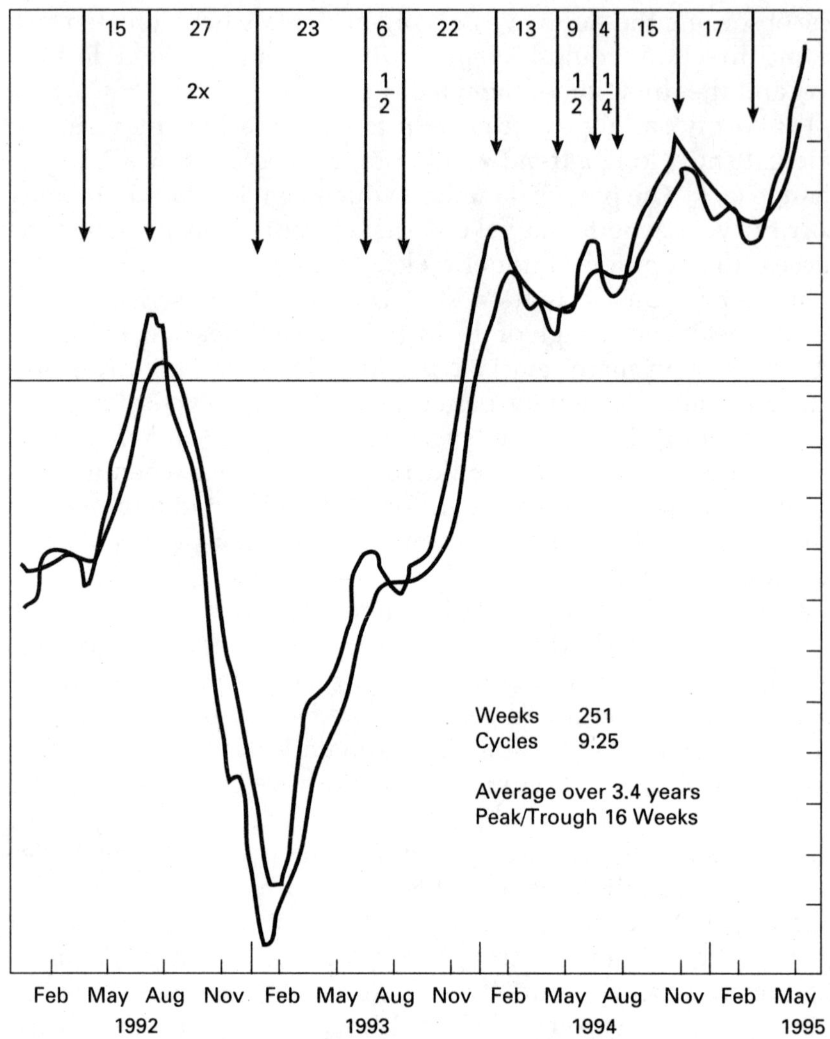

Graph 4-4. IBM weekly cycle from MACD peaks and troughs.

cycle waves means that there were only 9.25 full waves in the 151-week period, giving an average trend length of 16 weeks.

Once the average cycle wave length is identified and we already have identified the most recent peak or trough, then we can calculate how far we have progressed in the current trend. In our IBM example we identified the last weekly MACD trough as occurring on February 24. This means that on May 12 the market was 11 weeks into an average trend length of 16 weeks and was written on the worksheet as 11/16.

We could have used this calculation to forecast the next peak in 5 weeks' time on June 16, 1995, but forecasting is not part of this trading method (minor peak actually occurred May 26 or 13 weeks from trough—major peak was August 18). I use the calculation to reduce the input of the weekly values into the synergy equation.

First I add the weekly indicator values in the direction of weekly ROC. In Box 4-8 the MACD on ROC weekly direction was long. We had values of 4 for the moving average, of 3 for the MACD on price trough, and 4 for MACD on ROC—total 11.

I want to reduce the input of these factors by half the period that we are into the average trend. In the example this is the calculation:

Cycle-Adjusted Weighting
May 12, 1995

$$\text{Deduction} = \text{weekly values} \times 0.5 \times \frac{\text{weekly maturity}}{\text{average wave length}}$$

$$\text{Deduction} = 11 \times 0.5 \times {}^{11}\!/_{16} = -3.78$$

$$\text{Unadjusted weighting} = (B)2 + (B)4 + (B)2 + (T)3 + (T)1 + (T)4 + (T)2 = 18$$

$$\text{Adjusted weighting} = 18 - 3.78 = 14.22$$

Market	D	W	M	D	W	M	D	W	M	W M
Weight	2	4	2	1	3	1	1	4	2	20
IBM	B	B	B	P	T	T	S	T	T	11/18

Weight: = 14.2/20 = 71% long

Box 4-8.

$$\text{Deduction} = 11 \times 0.5 \times {}^{11}\!/_{16} = 3.78$$

$$\text{Previous total values} = 18$$

$$\text{Adjusted weighting} = 18 - 3.78 = 14.22$$

$$\text{New percentage} = 71\%$$

In this instance 11 weeks into a 16-week cycle wave reduced the chances of success from 90% to 71%.

This factor's value is seen when the cycle wave is nearing completion because it might keep one out of the market when using the Woodes Rogers strategy.

The cyclical factor is another way of reducing risk but of course it does keep one out of markets. If you are more adventurous, and able to handle increased risk, you might decide to modify this factor in your own calculations.

Trading the Woodes Rogers Strategy

I make one last simple calculation on my worksheet. I multiply the market synergy percentage by the ROC value on the day to produce my *Risk-Assessed Return Index*—RARI.

If the market is long 71% with a ROC of +104, the RARI is 0.71 × 104 = +74.

Both the synergy percentage and the ROC have to have the same positive or negative sign for a result, otherwise the RARI is neutral. For example,

$$\text{Short } 65\% \times -10 = -6.5$$

$$\text{Long } 50\% \times +20 = +10$$

$$\text{Long } 50\% \times -10 = -(\text{neutral})$$

$$\text{Short } 50\% \times +10 = -(\text{neutral})$$

The adjusted-weighting percentage and the RARI are the essence of all the previous calculations and the simple guide to my trading strategy.

Calculating RARI
(Risk-Assessed Return Index)

$$\text{RARI} = \text{FIRMROC} \times \text{weight }\%$$
$$= +104.5 \times +71\%$$
$$= +74$$

Positive × negative = neutral

$$\text{RARI} = +9.9 \times -62\%$$
$$= \text{neutral}$$

Box 4-9.

When the percentage is short above 65% and the RARI is in excess of −10, I wish to enter that market from the short side.

When the percentage is long above 65% and the RARI is in excess of + 10, I wish to enter that market from the long side.

When the above conditions change below the parameters, I wish to exit.

In one final sailing analogy, the percentage tells me from which direction my course should be from a wind that has a 65% + chance of remaining true and blowing above 10 knots (or miles per hour). When the wind becomes fluky or erratic or very light (low RARI), I don't like to compete. I also become cautious once the wind starts blowing above 60 knots (or the RARI goes above 60).

The actual entry and exit signal can be taken from charts on the day or from following the short-term advice of your broker. Other methods are discussed in following chapters. The preferred entry and exit are tactical.

One can also use an entry and/or exit calculated from the simple moving averages. Using the formula in Chapter 3, Box 3-10, one can calculate the crossover point of the 3- and 13-day moving averages on the high or the low price of the contract or stock to be traded. By placing a stop order at this calculated price, a conservative entry or exit can be made.

What I hope I have accomplished in this chapter is to demonstrate that it is possible to identify the markets in which the chances of success are greatest.

The work involved in the system is setting up the computer program and adjusting my template for your policy and markets. Once this is established, you will find that you can easily monitor 50 stocks and/or markets while trading in only five markets or fewer.

The calculations above on IBM told me on May 12, 1995, that if I was long on the stock, I should be looking closely at profit taking or reducing my position. If I was not in the stock I would be extremely cautious about buying. The relatively high RARI value, +74, and the maturity of the cycle move suggest that any tactical entry should be short term from the long side, and will be reasonably high risk. The more conservative trader would be looking to sell. After you read this, why not look at an IBM chart and see what happened after May 12, 1995.

You now have all the elements to become a conservative speculator who will become far more successful than that old privateer Woodes Rogers.

5

Tactics of Attack: Actions of a Daring Privateer

Henry Morgan—Daring Buccaneer

The strategy that I have just outlined should be sufficient to allow the trader with a conservative policy to commence trading as soon as he or she redefines the strategy to suit his or her resources. The Woodes Rogers strategy provides relaxed entry and exit points, using simple moving averages or charting techniques, for those traders who cannot monitor the markets throughout the trading day. The policy time frame of these traders is 1 to 12 weeks, and the strategy is designed to the limitations of one trading signal per day. The strategy works because a large number of markets are monitored by a sound, structured system to choose the best potential trades.

There have been many times when I have been operating the strategy that markets have had potential to make profits but the risk was heightened because a cycle peak or trough was due. At such times as maybe May 12, 1995, for IBM stock (see Chapter 4), the profitability of the strategy would have been enhanced by a short-term tactical method.

There are a number of traders who seek excitement in the markets, as well as profits. These traders often do not have the patience to stay out of a market for weeks, waiting for the best potential time to trade. They have a nearly biological need to be in a market most of the time. Without good tactics these excitement seekers do not last very long.

Tactics can be defined as the implementation of strategy. One can have a sound policy, and a superlative strategy, yet still suffer debilitating losses with terrible tactics. On the other hand, how many battles throughout history have been won simply by the daring tactics of a captain, despite the poor strategy given to him by his admirals? It is the daring tactics that are embellished by writers and which make popular heroes at the time of battles. Strategy is often only examined later by historians and war colleges, out of the public gaze.

Let me tell you a story of a daring pirate who became much more famous than the relatively conservative Woodes Rogers, because of his daring tactics on the Spanish Main.

The earliest buccaneers were sixteenth-century descendants of French refugees, English deserters, and stranded Dutch smugglers on the island of Hispaniola (now Haiti and the Dominican Republic). They survived on wild cattle and pigs, abandoned when the Spanish colonized the South American mainland. They traded dried smoked meat known as *viande boucanée* for guns and ammunition from seafaring adventurers. By the mid-seventeenth century the buccaneers had progressed from meat traders to coastal raiders, to become organized pirates who called themselves the Brethren of the Coast. In 1667 a Welshman named Henry Morgan was accepted by the Port Royal–based buccaneers as Admiral of the Confederation of the Brethren of the Coast.

Three hundred years before the twentieth-century war in Vietnam, a treaty was signed between England and Spain in May 1667, agreeing not to interfere in one another's trade. No mention in the vague treaty was made of America and the West Indies. The Governor of Jamaica, Sir Thomas Modyford, then became horrified when he received information of a possible Spanish invasion from the neighboring island of Cuba. Spain had long been concerned about the pirate havens in French-controlled Tortuga (Hispaniola) and English Port Royal (Jamaica).

The Spanish Main

Early voyages of discovery provided Spain with unprecedented riches from sixteenth-century colonies in the New World of the West Indies and South America. By exploiting native labor, the Spanish colonies were able to ship home silver from Peru, gold from Chile, emeralds from Venezuela, as well as transship through Mexico many oriental treasures from their colony in the Philippines. Mainland South America, particularly from the Isthmus of Panama to the mouth of the Orinoco River in Venezuela, became known as the Spanish Main.

Pirates, attracted by the riches which were flooding into Europe, established bases in the Bahamas and Lesser Antilles, surrounding Spanish bases in Cuba, Hispaniola, and Puerto Rico. Spain met the threat to the sea lanes from pirates by creating large convoys which formed in Havana and were made up of ships carrying treasures from Cartegena (Colombia), Portobelo (Panama), and Veracruz (Mexico).

French, Dutch, and English raiders responded by attacking the often poorly defended Spanish settlements on land.

The exploits of pirates taking Spanish prizes in the Caribbean and West Indies led to the whole area being called the Spanish Main.

Box 5-1.

In January 1668, Modyford commissioned Henry Morgan "to take prisoners of the Spanish nation, whereby he might inform of the intentions of that enemy to invade Jamaica." There was no real profit to privateers in simply taking prisoners, so Morgan and his captains decided to attack the Cuban town of Porto Principe. There was little strategy. Morgan assembled twelve ships and 700 men to storm the town, some fifty miles inland from Ana Maria Bay.

The hard-bitten buccaneers stormed the town, and were more than a match for Porto Principe's militia, who surrendered to save the town from being razed to the ground. When the spoils were divided, the men grumbled that 50 pieces of eight were insufficient reward for so much labor. Morgan decided to lead his Brethren to greater riches by attacking the mainland colony of Portobelo on the Caribbean coast of Darien, sixty miles north of the city of Panama.

There can be no questioning Morgan's daring. With his pirate fleet down to nine ships and 460 men, following the departure of his French buccaneer allies, Morgan planned to attack a fortified town that might be defended by heavy cannon and 1200 men. There is also no doubt of Morgan's motive. Portobelo was the port where bullion and other South American treasures were loaded for the convoy to Spain.

Morgan's strategy was to attack the three forts of San Felipe, Santiago de la Gloria, and San Jeronimo by land, after which Portobelo could be threatened by sea. The buccaneers rowed to the headland above the Gloria fortress from the fleet anchored thirty miles west of the town. The fort, untroubled for seventy years, was vulnerable to land attack, and fell quickly to the stealth of Morgan's men.

The next fort, San Jeronimo, to which the town's governor retreated with his family, appeared impregnable. It was surrounded by water and connected to land only by a causeway. Morgan's ruthless tactic was to advance behind a human shield of eighty priests and nuns, against which most Spanish soldiers would not fire. The tactics succeeded and the fort was secured, following the death of a number of servants of God, and the governor.

The fleet appeared off the harbor entrance, in sight of the fort of San Felipe, whose soldiers were not to know that the ships were manned with only skeleton crews. With a large contingent of buccaneers visibly ready to attack by land, and the fleet in view, the fort of San Felipe surrendered.

The plunder from Portobelo was reported to have been 250,000 pieces of eight, silks, silver plate, and 300 slaves. The reward was gained at the cost of eighteen English killed and thirty-five wounded.

Henry Morgan succeeded in his Portobelo enterprise despite acting outside his commission, by applying crude strategy and daring tactics. His buccaneer fleet was not the relatively disci-

Sir Henry Morgan

In 1669 Morgan tried a strategy similar to the one employed at Portobelo in attacking Spanish towns on the Venezuelan Lake of Maracaibo. At one stage he was bottled up by well-armed Spanish vessels, and another man of weaker will might well have surrendered. Morgan made good use of a "fireship" to destroy the enemy "men of war" barring his way, and then through subterfuge again escaped the defending fortress to share out the rich equivalent of £30 per man with his victorious privateers.

Henry Morgan's famous sacking of Panama in 1671 was a mercantile failure. Possibly through overconfidence, Morgan failed to gather sufficient intelligence and so suffered heavy losses in men and ships before he even arrived at Panama. Although Morgan was finally successful in sacking and burning "that famous and ancient city of Panama, which is the greatest mart of silver and gold in the whole world," the major wealth had already been dispatched from the city by treasure ship and mule train.

Morgan's excesses of his commission as privateer caused him later to be taken to London for trial. Influence from friends and changes of political fortune led Morgan not only to escape any trial, but to be knighted by King Charles II and appointed Deputy Governor of Jamaica.

As an economic side note, Sir Henry Morgan's instructions to return to Jamaica in 1674 were delivered by a clerk of the Board of Trade—John Locke, who in 1690 penned one of the first books on socioeconomics, the "Essay Concerning Human Understanding."

Box 5-2.

plined group that was later commanded by Woodes Rogers. Morgan's bloodthirsty pirates had to be given regular chances at obtaining booty or else his authority was lost. Morgan could not wait for the more opportune time to attack Portobelo when the treasure was being assembled for shipment to Spain. He grasped the opportunity of a loose commission and a limited victory at

Porto Principe to convince his gang of cutthroats to attempt a high-risk venture at Portobelo.

There is every chance that without the ruthless tactics employed the venture might have failed. The fort of Santiago de la Gloria was attacked from the headland and the entire garrison slaughtered. The attack on the fort of San Jeronimo succeeded only because of the use of human shields. The ruthlessness of seventeenth-century tactics should not be sentimentally judged with twentieth-century cultural intellect. There was little quarter given between enemies in the seventeenth century, and little respect by the Reformed English for servants of the Pope.

In my opinion Henry Morgan demonstrated that quick, bold tactics can succeed, despite poor strategy and policy.

Formulation of Technical Tactics for Speculation

As mentioned earlier, tactics can be defined as the implementation of strategy, but the point of my piratical tale is that tactics need not necessarily be *dependent* on strategy. Strategy can be formed in a relaxed time frame, but tactics often have to be implemented with urgency. We plan in weeks and days. We act in hours, minutes, and even microseconds.

It is my personal preference to have a tactical system that operates in accord with a structured strategy under the umbrella of a predetermined policy. Accordingly, the tactical system which I suggest is designed to implement the trades in the markets already identified by the Woodes Rogers strategy outlined in the previous chapter. The success of my FLASH system proves that trading with relaxed daily stops can work.

Henry Morgan Speculative Tactics

I believe that Henry Morgan had a crude strategy for his attack, but then relied on his daring and wit to adjust tactics during the course of battle.

My tactical plan for speculation in stocks and futures markets commences with a strategy that certain action in one or more markets can be expected to occur. Based on those expectations I can operate tactics to enter the market, to safeguard my new position, and to provide protection for other positions which might be considered vulnerable, until more relaxed strategic controls can be applied.

Woodes Rogers had the patience to sail halfway round the world to attack a major prize. Henry Morgan used his resources to attack targets of opportunity.

The strategy outlined in Chapter 4 was to wait for conditions when the system synergy was above 65% and the RARI above 10. I still recommend that this strategy be followed when the volatility of markets, as measured between day-to-day closes, is less than 0.8%. In fact, in such low-volatility markets, the moving-average signal alone often provides success.

In markets with a volatility above 0.8%, and particularly above 1% (reflecting an average daily movement of 0.8–1.0%+ of price), more aggressive action can be taken. The aim is aggressive entry at times when the conservative strategy might stay out of the market and then to safeguard that position until a decision to exit is made or until the position can be safeguarded by strategic stops. We can also use the tactical system to quit or lessen the strategic position in overbought or oversold markets, and then reenter once the correction has passed.

Direction

The direction of tactical entry is decided by the same factor that decides the strategic direction—the direction of the weekly ROC.

A tactical exit is just that—an exit. No direction of the market is necessarily assumed. We exit simply because our expectations are not being met.

Daily Rate of Change

The Woodes Rogers strategy used a daily rate-of-change indicator (FIRMROC) which indicated the momentum today compared to the price 55 days previously, expressed roughly as a percent per annum. But 55 days is too long a period for a system designed for quick action. The percentage per annum was used so that different markets could be compared. In tactics we are concerned only with the one market we intend to attack.

Accordingly, I have chosen the momentum indicator, which is standard on many technical analysis computer systems, and applied it to a 21-day period. I have then used the standard MACD format on the ROC data to produce a MACD line and Signal line.

When the 21-day momentum indicator, as indicated by the MACD crossover, is moving in the same direction as the weekly FIRMROC indicator, we will enter the market in that direction.

I have recently become aware that some technical analysis software programs do not allow the running of "studies on studies" such as the MACD study on a momentum study. Some programs allow only standard studies on price data. You will need to be selective about your software if you wish to follow this tactical system. I know that Computrac, its successor SMARTrader Professional, Windows SMARTrader, and the Windows version of Metastock do allow studies on studies.

Moving Average

The strategic price indicators were comprised of simple moving averages because I believe that the overall direction of the market is best viewed with simple averages. The energy of a daily market is, however, best judged with exponential moving averages, which place greater emphasis on most recent prices and less on historical values.

I continue to use the combination of a 3-day average and a 13-day average to provide the action signal. When the 3-day exponential moving average (EMA) of the daily *high* price moves up through the 13-day exponential moving-average *high*, and the daily ROC, in line with the weekly ROC, is rising, then I want to be long in that market.

When the 3-day exponential moving average of the daily *low* price moves down through the 13-day exponential moving-average *low*, and the daily ROC, in line with the weekly ROC, is falling, then I want to be short in that market.

Many computerized technical analysis systems generate mathematical indicators of the averages in addition to graphics. The 13-day exponential moving average can be used as an entry stop if the 3/13 crossover has not already occurred. If the crossover has already occurred, one can either conservatively wait for another signal, or take action immediately (at market or using chart analysis) and then use the 13-day exponential moving average as the exit stop.

A more conservative entry point would be the point where the daily price penetrated beyond the 13-day exponential moving average by a certain amount, called a filter. Rather than take the calculated 13-day EMA as the stop entry point, I can suggest the 13-day EMA *plus* a filter 1 percent of the calculated EMA price to buy, or *less* a filter 1 percent of the EMA price to sell. For example, if the 13-day EMA of the S&P 500 market highs was 611.5, one could look to buy at 617.6 (611.5 + 6.1). Alternatively, if the 13-day EMA of the S&P 500 market lows was 604.7, one could look to sell at 598.7 (604.7 − 6.0).

Another conservative entry point can be suggested by using the maximum failed penetration of the 13-day EMA in the last 90 days, rather than a percentage of the current EMA. The computer displays the calculated exponential moving averages overlaid on the daily Open/High/Low/Close. The past 90 days can be examined for past penetration of the 13-day EMA in the direction in which one is looking to act (as suggested by the 21-day momentum). The maximum penetration is then added to today's 13-day EMA when looking to buy, or deducted when looking to sell. For example, when looking to sell the S&P 500 we could find that there were three occasions in the past 90 days where the day's low had moved below the 13-day EMA (of the daily lows) and then rallied back to a bull trend above the EMA after one to four days. The penetrations (13-day EMA minus the daily low) might have been 6.3, 8.6, 5.2 points. Instead of looking to place the sell entry stop at the 13-day EMA of 604.7, the stop could be placed at 596.1 (604.7 − 8.6).

The various tactical actions are best understood with practical examples.

Simple Entry on Crossover

In the week ending February 3, 1995, the COMEX HG copper market (90-day perpetual contract) weekly FIRMROC signal turned bearish. The conservative trader might have waited for a daily rally, which commenced in mid-February and lasted until the end of March.

On March 31, 1995, the 21-day ROC MACD signal of the May 1995 Copper contract turned down through the Signal line (see Graph 5-1(*b*)). At the same time the 3-day exponential moving-average low was approaching the 13-day exponential moving average, which was mathematically indicated as 135.74.

The trader would place a sell stop to enter the market at or near 135.75 cents per pound on the next trading day, April 3 (after Easter). This order would have been unsuccessful but orders would have been placed on following days:

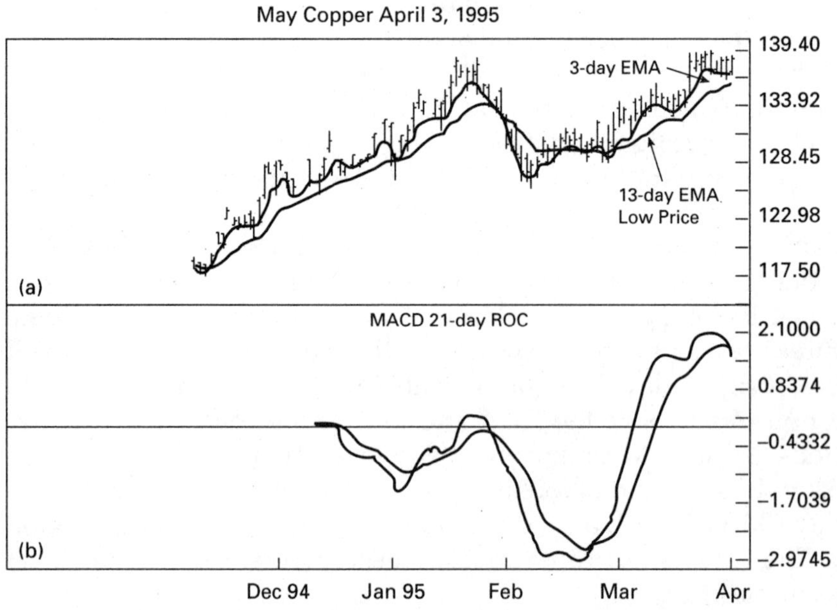

Graph 5-1. New York copper—conservative "Morgan" tactics.

April 4	135.95
April 5	136.10
April 6	136.15

The market on April 6 opened at 137.00 and fell to 135.80 before closing at 136.55. The entry point was at or near 136.15 on April 6.

An exit stop would then be used until the trade was liquidated, or until it was decided that a relaxed strategic stop would be sufficient. In fact the May contract could have been quit on April 26 at 126.00 cents per pound for a net profit of $2450 or 82% initial margin.

Aggressive Entry with Exit Stop

When the 90-day perpetual contract weekly FIRMROC of the copper contract turned down in the week of February 3, 1995, the daily moving averages had already crossed (Graph 5-2(*a*)). An aggressive trader might not like to wait for a rally before entering.

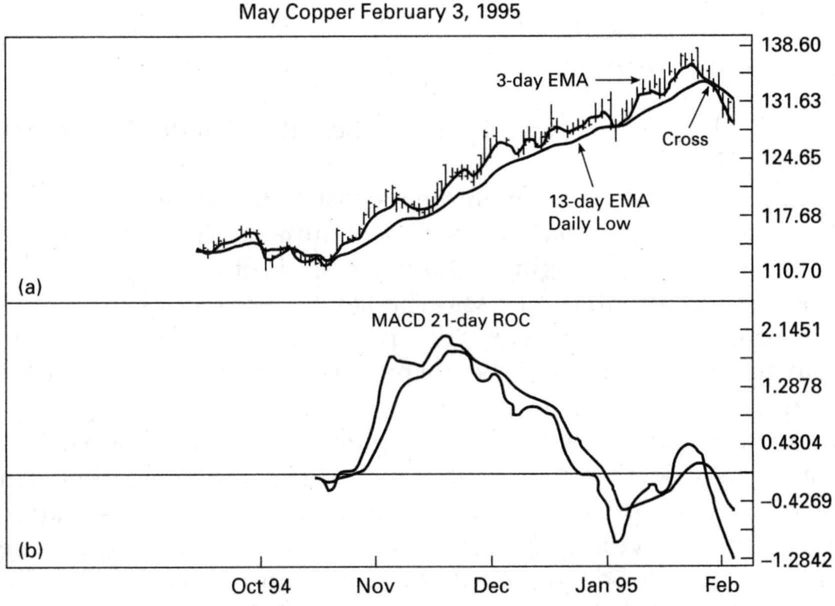

Graph 5-2. New York copper—aggressive "Morgan" tactics.

With daring tactics the aggressive trader could sell either on the opening on Monday, February 6, or at a chart level. Let's assume that he entered on or near the opening price on February 6:126.80.

Our aggressive trader knew that a rally was likely and so wanted to limit his losses with a relatively tight stop. On the day of entry, and for maybe two days after entry, I recommend that the exit stop be calculated on the closest 13-day exponential moving-average signal, which in this copper example would be the 13-day exponential moving average of the daily *low.* This means that on the day of entry, February 6, assuming an entry short on the opening, a stop would have been placed to buy if the price rose above 132.12 cents per pound.

The 13-day low exponential moving-average figure was also used as stops on:

February 9	132.65
February 10	132.15

The 13-day *high* exponential moving-average figure would be used as stops on:

February 13	132.00
February 14	131.70

The exit stop would have been touched at the high of February 14: 131.70.

The aggressive trader would have lost on this trade but limited losses to $1225 per contract, or 58% of initial margin of $2100.

Battles are not fought without blood. Profitable speculation does not occur without losses. The key to successful speculation is to ensure that the losses are small, but profits large—money management, which will be covered in more detail in the next chapter.

An aggressive trader will trade more often than a conservative trader because he or she wants to be in the market more often. An aggressive trader will suffer more losses than a conservative trader, but providing those losses are contained, the aggressive trader can still be successful. I am by nature conservative, so maybe I am biased in my observation that a conservative trader will experience the best monetary success. The aggressive trader often sacrifices some profits for excitement.

Profit-Taking Exit

In recent years many fund managers have blamed the poor performance of their funds on the so-called "unexpected" collapse of the U.S. T-Bond market. You have no doubt read the comments, not dissimilar to those which followed the 1987 stock market crash, that no one forecast the 1994 bond collapse. These comments should be interpreted to mean that "the crowd (psychology) was bullish and warning signals were ignored."

In fact the U.S. T-Bond market peaked in October 1993 (in the 36th month of a 39-month cycle phase). There was a rally from November 1993 until end of January 1994, before the second downward impulse started the slide which many market professionals failed to expect. The Woodes Rogers strategy signaled short positions in the week ending February 25, 1994, as per Graph 5-3. Furthermore the three simple moving averages 5-week, 13-week, and 34-week formed a cluster at the same time. As explained earlier, a *cluster* occurs when the three harmonic moving averages cross each other at approximately the same time. The cluster is a good confirming signal, so that in my speculative system, I am prepared to double the size of my standard entry trade.

It was possible to sell June 1994 T-Bonds on February 22, 1994, above 111$^{7}/_{32}$, so let's assume that you might have shorted at that price. Because the Woodes Rogers strategy was working, you would have been working a loose stop through March into April, but by Friday April 15 you would have noted that the T-Bond market was in week 26 of a 26-week cycle phase. You could have then used Henry Morgan tactics to look for a finely tuned exit stop.

Graph 5-4 illustrates the June 1995 T-Bond contract 3- and 13-day exponential moving averages on the high (Graph 5-4(*a*)) and the 21-day ROC (Graph 5-4(*b*)). It can be noted that the downward momentum or ROC had troughed in March, so that new positions should not have been added after that trough.

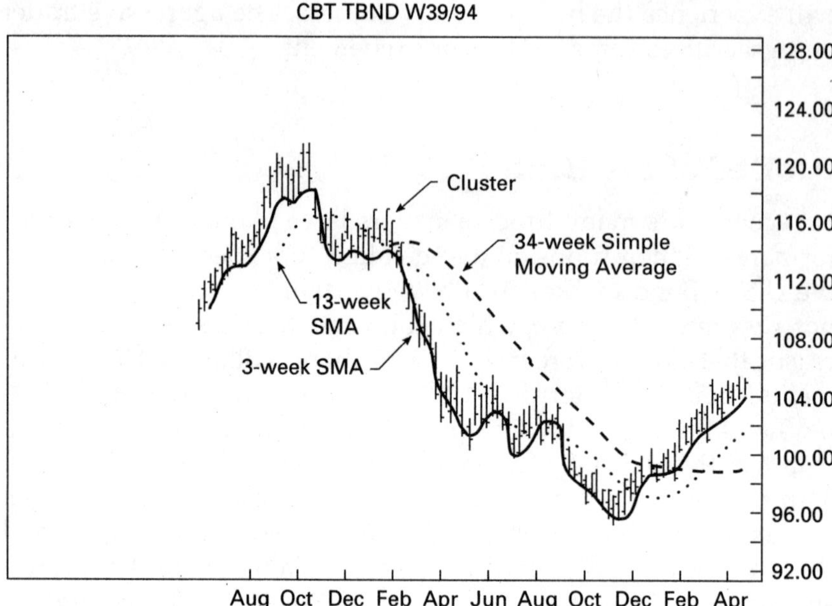

Graph 5-3. CBoT T-Bonds—"Rogers" strategic entry.

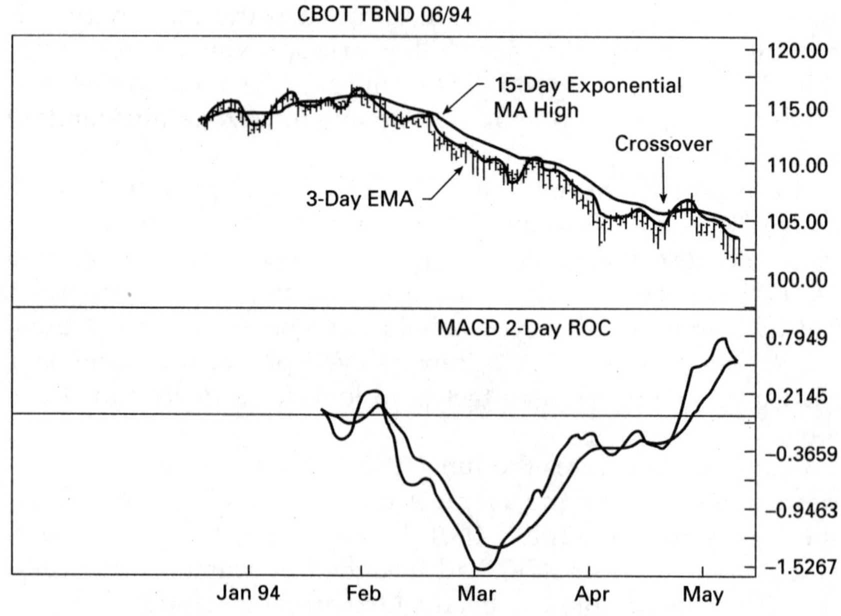

Graph 5-4. CBoT T-Bonds—"Morgan" tactical exit.

You could have commenced placing buy stops from April 18 using the exponential moving average of the 13-day high as the trigger.

April 18 $105^{06}/_{32}$
April 19 $105^{00}/_{32}$
April 20 $104^{18}/_{32}$
April 21 $104^{17}/_{32}$

The stop would have triggered on April 21 when the high was $105^{31}/_{32}$. The actual crossover of the 3- and 13-day exponential moving averages occurred the next day.

The selling price of $111^{7}/_{32}$ and buying price of $104^{17}/_{32}$ translate to a profit of $7762 per contract, or 300% on initial margin in 60 days.

Serial Trading

Graph 5-5 illustrates the differences between the exponential moving averages on the highs (Graph 5-5(*a*)) and lows (Graph 5-5(*b*)) of the Dow Jones Industrial Average. The buy signals are generated by a 13-day exponential moving average of the daily high, and sell signals by the 13-day exponential moving average of the daily low.

I don't advocate using one technical indicator on its own, but the signals generated in this illustration show that trading the stock market would have been profitable in the direction of the weekly FIRMROC.

December 14	Buy	DJIA 3751.0	
January 20	Sell	DJIA 3848.9	+97.9
February 3	Buy	DJIA 3895.1	
March 3	Sell	DJIA 3944.4	+49.3
March 9	Buy	DJIA 4007.3	
April 28	Value	DJIA 4321.3	+314.0

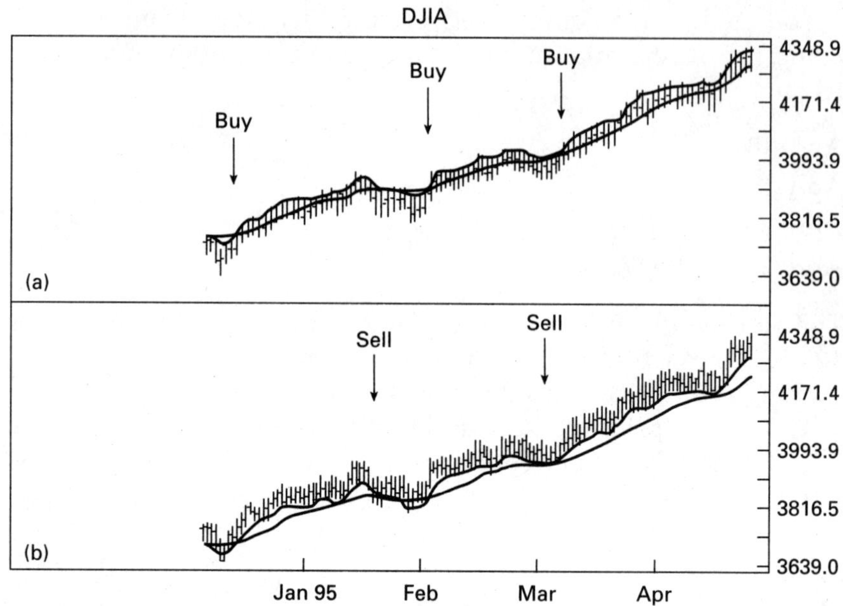

Graph 5-5. Dow Jones Industrial Average exponential averages.

I don't expect that everyone who reads this book will be willing or even able to undertake all the work necessary to follow the speculative systems that I have outlined. My experience has shown that many speculators are work shy. Those who are serious about making money in the markets now have indicators to form their own policy, strategy, and tactics, which will provide the basis of success. Using these indicators as battle intelligence, those who are willing to expend time to advantage will allow the markets to tell them when to attack to seek the rich prizes.

Even with the indicators, all trades are not profitable, so losses have to be limited. Limiting losses and enhancing profits is the role of risk management, which is the meat of the next chapter.

6

Exponential Money Management: Maximizing Profits and Controlling Risk

Now you have most of the elements to allow you to become a successful privateer speculator. Policy gives direction and purpose; strategy indicates which markets to attack and a conservative trading method; tactics provide daring entry and exits. The remaining element of the battle plan is the prudence not to commit your total attacking force in a single market raid.

You might recall that the conservative privateer Woodes Rogers sailed halfway around the world to attack a fabulously rich prize: the Manila Galleon. After attacks with part of his fleet against vastly superior firepower, he withdrew, to safeguard the treasure that he had already pillaged.

The buccaneer Henry Morgan succeeded in forcing the surrender of the last fort of Portobelo because he had kept the fleet in reserve, manned by a skeleton crew. For all the daring of the pirates of old, they had the prudence to keep forces in reserve, and to know to withdraw when the odds were not in their favor.

When speculating in the market, this prudence of privateers and pirates becomes the metaphor for the element of money management. A sound money management plan is the most important element of success, after strategic and tactical discipline. Money management recognizes that markets can at any time suddenly reverse direction due to an unseen event which can turn profits into disastrous losses.

In the thirty years that I have been associated with trading markets, I have noticed one constant factor—that the majority of futures speculators lose. The losing percentage is generally quoted at around 75%. This means that people are continually attracted by the high rewards of leveraged futures trading, but that 75% of those intrepid souls will lose any money committed to the markets. I have not had a long association with stock market speculators, but suspect that a similar percentage of losers could be found.

What is not often mentioned by futures brokers is that the successful 25% of speculators tend to be the people who learned the secrets of money management early, so that they outlasted all of the new people trying their luck at speculation. So, in terms of numbers, over the years the losing speculators as a percentage of total participants is a number far higher than 75%—because of the huge turnover of losers. The winning percentage is a relatively minuscule number of people who continually follow well-managed trading plans.

In my experience, the most common mistake that speculators make is to commit too much of their fund pool to single trades. As a broker I used to advise that the minimum amount needed to cover a trade was 3 times the initial margin. This was often considered conservative by excitement seekers, who then, by not following my advice, philosophically took their losses and departed the trading scene. They tended to act in much the same way as losing punters who leave the racetrack mentally stimulated but financially poorer.

Some professional fund managers suggest that trading with 33% of funds is not conservative. One well-known managed fund trades with only 25% of available funds, so that 75% is always kept in reserve. This allows this successful fund to guarantee that, despite trading highly leveraged markets, there will not be any further call on capital. However, the low percentage of funds they commit, while trading in high-risk markets, ensures that the return on total funds is, in my opinion, inadequate.

The reason that funds need to be kept in reserve is to allow the speculator to take losses, but still have sufficient capital to trade again to more than recoup earlier losses. Relatively large reserves are kept to cover sequential losses. A sequence of losing trades is inevitable at some time unless the trading plan is far superior to any that I have discovered.

I consider the Woodes Rogers strategy to be conservatively successful with a win/loss ratio of approximately 1.4:1. This means that over a 2-year period there were 1.4 times more winning trades than losing trades. Even with this strategy, there was a sequence of nine losing trades in 1993.

The American trading psychologist Dr. Van K. Tharp in his preliminary seminars suggests that, in a random walk system, the sequence of losing trades can be as high as 16. This would mean that, to have any chance of success, the trader would have to withstand 16 losses in a row, and still have sufficient capital to trade the seventeenth time. If the trader was trading one contract and could contain losses to the value of the initial margin, then for each trade, 16 times the initial margin should be kept in reserve. If one wanted to trade four futures contracts at a time, then reserves would need to be 64 times the contract initial margin. Unfortunately, the return on total funds with that size reserves is likely to be much too low to have appeal to speculators.

Before I give my method of money management, I should also indicate again that there are more mathematically detailed methods suggested in books by Ralph Vince and N. J. Balsara, to mention just two. Before you establish the money management technique to suit your own policy, various methods should be examined.

Risk Management Parameters

My initial approach to money management was relatively simple. I wanted to trade a multiple number of contracts which would allow me the flexibility of reducing risk exposure without quitting a trade entirely. I believed that my trading system would produce at least a 50:50 chance of success and that I wanted to be able to trade up to five markets at one time. I simply calculated that I would need funds of 4 × 5 or 20 times the maximum initial margin of my chosen markets. In round figures, 20 × $5000 or $100,000 should allow me to trade four contracts in most markets chosen by the Woodes Rogers strategy.

I never made any allowance for a sequence of losing trades. My policy of taking partial profits in windfall trades and reducing losing positions meant that my average position was less than four, and closer to two, contracts. My policy of trying to trade simultaneously in diverse markets meant that, even if I was trading the maximum number of markets, losses were unlikely to occur in all five markets. If I was unlucky, losses might happen in three out of five. So in practice my maximum loss was limited to 2 × 3 or 6 times a median initial margin of $3000 to $18,000. Even though I did not allow for a losing sequence, I could in fact withstand a string of five large losses.

This initial approach, based on a number of contracts, was relatively standard in my broking experience. Individuals often had a standard trade of 1 or 10 contracts. Institutions and funds traded standard lots of 50 or 100 contracts.

The choice of lot size, higher or lower than standard, would often depend on whether the previous trade had made a profit or a loss, which in turn depends upon the personality of the trader. An aggressive trader might increase the lot size following a loss because of the optimistic desire to recoup. A conservative trader might reduce the trade size because of loss of confidence. Both traders would most likely change the trade size, because of the change in capital caused by the loss. The lot size might also be altered following a reasonable profit. This suggested that a trade size based on percentage of capital might be a better approach than one simply based on a number of contracts.

The first factor which I reexamined was my standard trade size. As a trend follower, I am really satisfied to be fully committed to the market when the trend is fully underway. In terms of the Woodes Rogers strategy this meant that I would consider the trend fully underway when the monthly moving average and monthly ROC signals were fully trending in my direction. I initiated my first risk management parameter by specifying that my

Risk Management Parameter 1

Trend	Moving-average indicator	ROC indicator	Percentage of standard
Rising	Bought	Sold	50
Rising	Bought	Bought	100
Falling	Sold	Bought	50
Falling	Sold	Sold	100

Box 6-1.

entry would be a percentage of the standard size according to the alignment of the monthly trading signals as per Box 6-1.

The effect of parameter 1 was to ensure that I was fully committed to the market when all Woodes Rogers indicators suggested high chances of success. On the other hand, I kept more in reserve when indicators were not so favorable.

In line with this philosophy I introduced my adventurous parameter 2, which is to allow double the parameter 1 position when a moving-average cluster is formed (see Chapter 3 on technical analysis).

I then calculated that parameter 1 reduced my maximum loss risk from $18,000 to $12,000 and reduced this dollar figure to a percentage of $100,000 capital. In this manner I calculated my standard trade size as 12% of equity. After three years of testing the Woodes Rogers trading strategy, I am still happy to have a standard trade size entry initial margin of 12% equity. Equity, not capital!

I define *equity* as the cash reserves remaining from capital after all profits, losses, initial margin, and maintenance margin have been taken into account. This means that once I have taken the first trade at the number of contracts whose initial margin represented 12% of capital, each subsequent standard trade is a lesser percentage of capital, but a standard position of equity. Such a standard trade policy increases the trading level exponentially following a string of profits, yet reduces exposure following losses.

In conjunction with the stop-losses of the Woodes Rogers strategy, the standard trade of 12% equity has allowed a maximum profit of 30.6% capital, maximum loss of 8.1% capital, while suffering a maximum drawdown of 30% capital. For those not familiar with futures terms, the maximum drawdown includes the maximum sequence of losses, as well as maintenance margins.

The unusually good result of the FLASH system in 1993 (see Box 4-3) was assisted greatly when capital was practically tripled in May, assisted by a $162,900 profit from a 16-contract London Metals Exchange (LME) copper position. This meant that the number of contracts traded enjoyed an exponential increase, later allowing a 55-contract position in London International Financial Futures Exchange (LIFFE) long gilt and subsequently a 140-contract position in New York Cotton Exchange (NYCE) cotton.

All my risk management research has been based on futures markets, which have high leverage. Those trading other derivatives, or less highly leveraged stock markets, need to do their own research on their preferred markets. In any case, even futures traders should not blindly follow my 12% equity standard. I believe that this risk management parameter will prove successful for the majority of traders following the Woodes Rogers strategy and Henry Morgan tactics in most markets. However, I cannot guarantee success. You must make your own calculations to have the confidence to take responsibility for your own actions.

I mentioned earlier that diversity of markets meant reduced risk. I do not have any standard groupings of markets which are considered similar, because the factors which influence markets vary over time. Some markets are obviously related, like IMM Eurodollars and IMM T-Bills, or stocks like IBM and Compaq. At times some markets are influenced by a factor such as interest rates, while at other times the same markets react differently. The S&P 500 at times will slavishly follow T-Bonds, but at other times surge in the opposite direction. Silver is a schizophrenic metal which can capriciously follow the trends of either precious metals or base metals.

I can't give you any standard group list, but will give you the guideline that markets which are subject to immediate reversal should a single fundamental factor change dramatically can be considered a group. For instance, in May 1995, in a climate of interest rate euphoria, a bad U.S. Consumer Price Index (CPI) figure would have reversed Eurodollars, T-Bills, T-Bonds, and to a lesser degree stocks and stock market indices. A good CPI would have been expected to put pressure on currency markets and precious metals. Going into the release of the CPI figure, one would not have wished to be overexposed in either of those groups.

Parameter 3 in my method of risk management is that the total open position in any group of closely related markets should not exceed 24% of capital. Capital, not equity!

The initial margins of two standard trades might add up to 24% of equity, but be below 24% of capital. Subsequent maintenance margins might increase the amount of funds committed to those related markets, up to 24% of capital. At such a level, my parameter 3 rule means that one or the other market position must be reduced, regardless of my strategy or optimistic outlook. The need to minimize risk exposure is much more important than the desire to optimize the return from a favorable trade. This is what money management is about—having the discipline to take an unpopular action to safeguard against the unthinkable.

Parameter 4 has not been exercised since I have been testing the trading system. Parameter 4 is that total market position, including initial and maintenance margins, should not exceed 72% of capital. This allows some reserves always to be kept to cover unforeseen events. The 72% figure is high by most standards of funds management, but is necessary if a target rate of return of 50% per annum in leveraged markets is to be achieved. I mentioned earlier that some funds will trade with only 25% of capital. I consider this too low. More standard is a 50% limit. The stop-losses generated by the strategy and tactics outlined earlier allow me to keep to a relatively high parameter. You must reach your own conclusions, based on your own trading plan.

Stop Orders

The key to committed risk management is stop-loss, stop-profit, and stop-entry orders, collectively known simply as "stops." Stops were defined in Chapter 2 on policy, and have been mentioned in

Parameters

Rules should never be broken. The parameter constant can be varied, but only with good reason.

1. Position percentage of standard is 50–100% according to monthly trading signals. Standard position is 12% equity.
2. Position as per parameter 1 can be doubled if moving-average cluster occurs simultaneously with entry. If no position allowed due to parameter 1, 25% of standard position can be taken on cluster only.
3. Position in individual or closely related markets is not to exceed 24% current capital.
4. Total position is not to exceed 72% current capital.
5. Tactical trading rules are to be followed until synergy percentage greater than 65% and RARI above +10 or below −10.

Box 6-2.

Chapter 4 on strategy and Chapter 5 on tactics. The technical methods that I have demonstrated are based on the premise that the trader does not have the time or resources to closely monitor the markets throughout the trading sessions.

Many market professionals criticize the use of stops, and indeed many floor traders seek to touch off stops. I can recall that locals would look for the stops recommended by Merrill Lynch during the silver boom of the late 1970s. Once the stop level was reached, "the thundering herd" stampeded temporarily while orders were filled that had instantly become "buy and repent, but buy." If the scalpers could take a position before the stampede, they could take profits during the stampede.

I don't believe that major brokers still recommend standard stops to their clients in the 1990s, but there is no doubt that the floor traders' search for large stop-order levels continues. Obvious chart stop points, such as the previous day's high or low, have an attraction to both the crowd and scalpers, for opposite reasons.

Because a stop-loss order becomes an "at-market" order when the stop price is triggered, placing the stop-loss does not guarantee that the order will be executed at the price specified, even though the market trades at the stop-loss price. If the market is moving quickly and passes through the stop before the broker has a chance to execute the order, the price at which the stop-loss order is executed may be higher or lower than the ordered price.

This is particularly relevant in international markets, since the prime determinants of price often tend to be those movements in U.S. markets which take place outside the trading hours of regional markets. Many times the Tokyo Nikkei, Sydney SPI, and London FT 100 stock index markets have opened sharply higher or lower following a large movement in the DJIA.

The alternative to entering a straight stop order is to enter a *stop limit order,* which becomes a normal limit order when the stop price is touched. The risk here (if this order is acceptable to the market) is that, if the market price continues to rise or fall without returning to the limit, the trader has the problem of a growing loss—the exact problem which she or he sought to avoid by placing the stop limit order.

I accept the criticism of stops, but the shortcomings of this type of order are far outweighed by the risk of loss without them. Those who cannot monitor the market closely need to employ stops to ensure long-term gain, and thus must endure the occasional short-term false reversal. This is the financial blood which must flow in the battles of the marketplace. Risk management simply tries to keep the loss of blood to a minimum. Rarely are there bloodless battles.

The amount of loss that the trader is willing to risk can be determined from a price level indicated by chart analysis if a technical system is used to trade. It can also be a percentage of the current price level or nothing more elaborate than the monetary loss the trader is willing to take before abandoning the trade.

The stops which follow are my suggestions of those to be employed to ensure that false reversals are minimized, risk also minimized, but profits protected.

Entry Stops

1. The Henry Morgan tactical entry is based on the crossover of the 3-and 13-day combination of exponential moving averages of the market's daily high or low, in combination with momentum indicators (possibly with conservative filter). This stop is designed to take a position as close to the market as possible, to take advantage of rises or falls which might develop into longer-term trends. A trade from this stop needs to be defended by another short-term stop until the longer-term trend move is confirmed.
2. The Woodes Rogers strategic entry is based on the crossover of the 3- and 13-day simple moving averages of the market's daily high or low, once other strategic criteria have been met. This stop is designed to take a position once the trend and impetus of the market have been identified. A trade from this stop can be defended by a similar relaxed stop, until the impetus can be seen to fade, when a shorter-term exit stop might be used.

Money Management Stops

Money management stops are not related to the trend in the market, but are designed to keep any losses to a minimum through periods of temporary upheaval. I believe that money management stops still need to be related to current market conditions, so use the recent market range to calculate the stop.

1. I have already mentioned that I measure a market's volatility by calculating the average daily movement from close to close (disregarding whether the day's movement is positive or negative). Volatility is then the average daily movement divided by the average daily closing price (basically over a 13-day period).

The average daily movement can be used to create a stop when the exit stop from simple moving averages might appear uncomfortably far away from the daily price. Three times the average daily movement can be considered unusual, and so provides the philosophical grounds for a money management stop. Because the stop is based on closing prices it should be valid on the close only.

When safeguarding a *long* position, 3 times the average daily movement should be *deducted* from the closing price, and the resultant calculated price entered as a stop close-only order.

When safeguarding a *short* position, 3 times the average daily movement should be *added* to the closing price, and the resultant stop price entered as a stop close-only order.

This stop should be entered only if the calculated market exit stop is out of range.

2. Another measure of the market's movement can be taken from the true range, which is basically the greater of the day's high/low range or the previous day's close to the high/low. An average true range can be calculated by averaging the daily true range over 13 days.

The average true range can be used to create a stop when the exit stop from exponential moving averages might appear uncomfortably far away from the daily price. Three times the average true range can be considered a surge or collapse which might signal a change in circumstances. Because this stop is based on the high/low range, it should be valid on a high or low. It is my choice to designate high or low of the previous 3 days from which to base the stop.

When safeguarding a *long* position, 3 times the average true range should be *deducted* from the highest price of the previous 3 days, and the resultant stop price entered valid for the day.

When safeguarding a *short* position, 3 times the average true range should be *added* to the lowest price of the previous 3 days and the resultant stop price entered valid for the day.

The stop should be entered only if the calculated market exit stop is out of range.

Exit Stops

1. The Henry Morgan tactical exit is based on the crossover of the 3- and 13-day combination of exponential moving averages of the market's daily high or low.
   a. To protect a *long* position immediately after entry, or when the momentum signal indicates a change of trend, the stop can be the 13-day exponential moving average of the *high*, providing

that the difference between the previous day's close and the stop exceeds the true range.

b. To protect a long position when conditions in item *a* above are not met and when strategic conditions are not met, the stop can be the 13-day exponential moving average of the daily *low.*

c. To protect a *short* position immediately after entry, or when the momentum signal indicates a change of trend, the stop can be the 13-day exponential moving average of the *low,* providing that the difference between the previous day's close and the stop exceeds the true range.

d. To protect a short position when conditions in item *c* are not met or when strategic conditions are not met, the stop can be the 13-day exponential moving average of the daily *high.*

2. The Woodes Rogers strategic exit is based on the crossover of the 3- and 13-day combination of simple moving averages of the market's daily high or low. Should the impetus of the trend be seen to fade (as measured by the synergy percentage and/or RARI), then an exit stop can be chosen from the previous short-term stops, i.e., those given by items 1*a* through 1*d*.

Stops

1. Tactical entry stop is limited to amount above/below previous close calculated by adding/subtracting 3 times the daily average price movement close-to-close.
2. Tactical entry stop is protected by tactical exit stop until strategic parameters allow strategic exit stop.
3. Money management stops, if closer to the market price, take precedence over exit stops.

Box 6-3.

Reentry after Stops

Although not a factor in risk management, I need to mention reentry after stops because it is extremely important in seeking profits. There is a natural tendency in traders to be wary of reentry into a market that has just been stopped out at a loss. I have learned to my cost that this natural tendency needs to be overcome, and that a quick reentry (according to your system parameters) more often than not results in good profits.

As mentioned earlier, stop orders are imperfect and have a tendency to be touched, for risk management purposes, just before the adverse move has run its course. As will be seen in the next chapter, constant monitoring of markets can be more efficient in avoiding false stops, but not everyone can be a professional trader. The stops which I have designed above will not avoid all false stops, but when false stops do occur under this system the subsequent reversal is often spectacularly profitable. There is no way that your natural sentiment can be denied, but I hope that you will quickly learn to overcome any negative sentiment and reenter as soon as the system parameters allow.

Rules

Unlike parameters, rules should not be adjusted and should be obeyed at all times.

Remember the adage of undersea divers quoted in Chapter 1: "Plan your dive. Dive your plan."? A good example of this sort of planning is provided by a dive from an island just off the coast of Australia which is surrounded by a marine sanctuary on the Great Barrier Reef. The diving is among the best in the world from a boat, but can also be enjoyed by taking advantage of the tide. The outgoing tide moves very fast from Heron Island and can take divers as much as three miles out to sea. Following the ebb, the incoming tide returns divers to the island over the colorful fish, coral, and sea creatures.

With the proper equipment and a properly timed diving plan, one can cover a huge area of reef viewing relatively safely. Without a proper plan, or if they depart from the plan to try to swim against the tide, the divers will need to be rescued. It is many years since I experienced the glories of this dive, and in those days the chances of rescue, in case of mischance, were slight. Even today, in the era of helicopter searches, it is critical to remember the diver's adage.

Trading the markets to take advantage of the flow of trends can be extremely profitable if the trading plan is sound. It is essential that any well-thought-out plan be followed completely. In the elements of trading systems and money management which I have introduced earlier, I have endeavored to make varying conditions, within rigid guidelines, to trade fluctuating but trending markets. The major rule which I can offer is that the guidelines must be rigidly observed, particularly in the case of money management stops. Do not use your forecasting ability to change stops, to try to anticipate market action. *Plan your trade; trade your plan.*

I use a secondary rule which can be helpful if you choose to monitor the markets in a similar manner. I monitor a market through a perpetual contract—either a spot contract or a 90-day perpetual contract, or both—and collect data only on an individual contract month when I am preparing to trade. Although I prefer the perpetual contract provided by CSI Inc., other data services have their own version of a continuous contract. When preparing to trade, I operate the computer programs over both the perpetual contract and the chosen contract month. In most instances the individual patterns of the perpetual and contract month are closely similar. Occasionally the patterns are different. It is my secondary rule never to take a position in a contract month if the patterns are different from those of the perpetual contract.

All the risk management terms that I have outlined are designed for trading markets for time periods of 3 to 90 days. Trading for short periods, e.g., day trading, requires new rules and new skills. In my opinion, short-term traders and scalpers are the real pirates of the markets.

7

Day Traders: The True Pirates

I believe that you, the reader, now have the elements to create your own profitable speculative trading system. No one else can do this for you. Speculation is one area of life in which, to be successful, you must take responsibility for your own actions. I hope that I have shown you that the signs for future market activity can be recognized from past and present market action. If you have the discipline to follow a system with sound basic elements, you will never blame the market for losses, and will rightly be able to be proud of your own success.

It would be remiss of me, however, to fail to recognize that many people do not have the personality to accomplish systematic trading. These are the true adventurers, who derive a great deal of enjoyment from trading in the markets minute to minute, pitting their wits against the unseen hand of the market crowd. Many of these excitement seekers are professional traders, although after thirty years in the markets, I can suggest that some "professional traders" are as "professional" as "common sense" is "common."

Billions of dollars change hands daily on international market floors and over the trading-computer "information superhighway." It is the size of the trading transactions by many professional traders that makes their name, not their approach to trading, or, on occasion, their discipline.

Barings Bank's Nick Leeson has been called a "rogue trader," but I have known other "professional traders" who have acted unprofessionally by falling in love with a trading position, against all odds. On the other side of the coin, there are eminent professionals like George Soros, who is a highly successful funds manager with well-publicized wins and losses to his credit. The book *Market Wizards* by Jack Schwager documents the exploits of a number of successful professional traders, and I have met a number of pit traders who have plied their profession successfully for many years.

How can the semi-professional trader looking for excitement emulate the successful professional traders? Not surprisingly, because my personality needs the discipline of systematic trading, I suggest that short-term trading can be successful only if a structured system is used. I shall suggest some computer methods and trading tips which, if practiced properly through constant trading, can become part of your trading method, which some years hence might not be viewed as systematic.

In the golden age of piracy, there were many pirates, but only a few have entered the annals of history. While some were strategists, like Woodes Rogers, many were simply good fighters, who practiced their swordplay and gunnery to enhance the chances of individual survival. Successful pirate captains were elected by the general body of pirates in a democratic manner, but only the strong held their position for a length of time, through continued success and personal fighting prowess. For example, the legendary Blackbeard is now thought to have commanded respect from his crew of cutthroats because he had a relatively huge physique and carried a number of loaded pistols, as well as cutlass and knives.

In the trading culture of the 1990s, the computer is the sharp weapon which has allowed a number of traders to watch the tick-by-tick trading of markets on the computer screen. These traders, often called "professional" because they trade full time, pit their wits against other professional traders on the market floor, as well as others using computer screens. Many of these traders trade large numbers of shares or futures contracts because they do not intend to carry the trade past the close of the trading session. These are the true day traders or scalpers, who are the modern equivalent of pirates involved in hand-to-hand fighting. Unlike the pirates, who didn't battle regularly, most day traders try to trade the markets daily. Day-to-day combat, while exciting, can be extremely debilitating and thus causes a high turnover as traders are knocked out of the market suffering from severe financial injuries.

Other traders have time frames of from 3 hours to 5 days. These traders often have access to large funds, but have strict management-imposed loss limits, particularly on overnight positions. The policy of these traders is to turn over the funds quickly and profitably, utilizing the computer power that large companies and banks have available. This form of short-term trading entails fewer casualties than intraday scalping, and the turnover of traders is less.

It is my opinion that excitement seekers should at least try to gain their short-term trading "sea legs," by operating with a time frame of 3 hours to 5 days, before they try minute-to-minute action.

Technical Method for Short-Term Speculation

Essentially the short-term tactical system is the same as the Henry Morgan tactics described in Chapter 5, with a reduced time frame. In addition to professional and semi-professional traders, this tactical system could appeal to the large numbers of retired people whose policy is to allow some of their portfolio to be used for speculation, but not enough to trade simultaneously in a number of markets. With only, say, $20,000 available, and an on-line signal to their computer, these people have the time to monitor the market reasonably closely, so can use more refined tactics than the daily Henry Morgan system.

I mentioned earlier my observations that any successful technical system should be able to work in any time frame. If you have a daily system of your own, test it with monthly, weekly, and hourly data. A well-constructed system will show similar success in all time frames. If the degree of success is disparate, try to find the flaw in the losing time frame and adjust the system.

The adjustment will often improve the system's operation in the standard time frame. Simplistically, my choice of preferred moving averages in the strategic context (i.e., 3- and 13-period) was proven separately over monthly, weekly, and daily data.

The philosophy behind the Woodes Rogers technical strategy (Chapter 4) was to use the synergy of three technical indicators over three time frames to target (and possibly trade) the markets and/or stocks with best potential in accord with the resources and goals of the trader's policy. The actual entry and exit points for trades could be fine-tuned by using the Henry Morgan tactics (Chapter 5), which used two indicators in the daily time frame in accord with one indicator from the weekly time frame.

I have spasmodically tested short-term trading systems since 1986, when a client who had previously agreed to follow my strategic system suddenly decided that he did not wish to hold overnight positions. Because publicly available on-line computer systems were not then freely available, my search for a short-term system depended on rapid hand-held calculations. The research proved costly to the client, who then withdrew from the market entirely and thus missed the huge short-term and intermediate-term profits from the 1987 stock market boom. Both the short-term and intermediate-term system were short on the SFE for the October 1987 crash when the Sydney market collapsed sharply.

In theory we should be able to use the same strategy and tactics over shorter time frames to provide profitable results. In fact I have tested the strategy over hourly, daily, and weekly data to choose markets in which to trade, but in practice the number of markets with good potential is limited. It is not only the trending nature of markets which is important in short-term trading but the momentum/volatility and the session times.

Relative Value of Markets

Many professional traders do not have much choice as to the markets they trade. Bond traders trade T-Bonds. Chicago Mercantile Exchange locals trade S&P 500 futures. These traders have to rely on their training to trade one market on both good days and bad days. I have suggested to management clients that their treasury would be more profitable if they allowed traders to skip trading on days when markets were listless, but this unconventional advice was not received with approval. To many managers, if traders don't trade, they are not working, and the work ethic overshadows any recognition that traders "speculate" (or whatever euphemism is used to cover up corporate speculation). My own experience managing traders is that error losses are most frequent on listless trading days, possibly because there is no adrenalin to stimulate good trading instincts. Those professional traders who trade only one market constantly and successfully have my admiration, and do not need recommendations from this book.

Traders who can choose their markets will need to pick markets which have a high tick value relative to the initial margin, as well as a reasonable trading range. The S&P 500 futures market, which is one of the most popular markets for short-term traders, in fact offered little value in my eyes in May 1995 because the initial margin of $31,250 was high compared to a tick value of $5. If I am to risk $31,250 overnight, I need a potential of 6250 ticks movement simply to give even-money odds. On May 2, 1995, the 13-day average true range of the S&P 500 Index was 340 ticks, which would mean that it might take me 18 days of average movement in my direction to make $31,250 profit. This thinking might not figure in the calculations of a scalper who doesn't necessarily carry a position overnight, but it is important to a trader with a time frame of 3 hours to 5 days.

I recommend that speculators widen their horizons by investigating international markets, which often have greater profit potential than U.S. markets. This is a policy decision. I use a standard formula to give a Value Index for markets which I wish to trade.

$$\text{Value Index} = \frac{\text{tick value}}{\text{initial margin}} \times \text{average true range}$$

True range is a standard option in a number of technical systems, and is defined by J. Welles Wilder (*New Concepts in Trading Systems*) as the greatest of:

1. The distance from today's high to today's low
2. The distance from yesterday's close to today's high
3. The distance from yesterday's close to today's low

In line with my attraction to Fibonacci numbers, the *average true range* in my formula is the true range averaged simply over 13 days.

The May 1995 S&P 500 example would give this calculation:

$$\text{Value Index} = \frac{\$5}{\$31{,}250} \times 365 = 0.0584$$

On the other hand the Chicago Board of Trade (CBoT) soy oil contract was calculated at the same time as follows:

$$\text{Value Index} = \frac{\$6}{\$675} \times 43 = 0.3822$$

Obviously, a Value Index of *0.38* suggests a market with more potential than one with a Value Index of *0.06*.

Box 7-1 gives an example of 17 popular U.S. futures contracts with calculations of a Value Index. Well, not all are popular. I have included the Australian dollar IMM contract, which does have low volume, but often presents good value for those with an international outlook. The calculations need to be carried out (on your computer) regularly because the Exchanges now change the initial margins relatively frequently. Exchanges use more sophisticated methods to calculate initial margins which truly cover current risk, but the principle is the same as my method of examining value.

It is my observation that a U.S. market with a Value Index much above 0.35 for any period can probably be expected to encounter a rise in initial margin. A market with a Value Index below 0.1 is likely to show conditions which might encourage the clearinghouse to ease initial margin conditions. I suspect that the continuing low Value Index of the S&P 500 futures contract is due to pressure from outside the CME to have a relatively high initial margin to deter public speculation.

International Exchanges with the exception of Japan do not enjoy the volume of U.S. trading, so occasionally can take a slightly more relaxed view on risk cover. Box 7-2 gives examples

Popular U.S. Futures Markets Average True Range Value Index

MAY 5, 1995

Market	Tick	Initial margin	13-day ATR	Value Index
IMM AUD/USD	$10.00	1,181	47	0.40
CBoT soy oil	$ 6.00	675	43	0.38
CBoT wheat	$ 6.25	845	45	0.35
IMM DEM/USD	$12.50	3,715	94	0.32
CBoT beans	$ 6.25	1,012	51	0.31
IMM Eurodoll	$25.00	760	9	0.30
CBoT T-Bond	$31.30	2,954	26	0.29
IMM CHF/USD	$12.50	5,735	129	0.28
NY sugar	$11.20	1,050	25	0.27
IMM JPY/USD	$12.50	7,595	161	0.26
IMM GBP/USD	$ 6.25	4,050	143	0.22
CMX silver	$ 5.00	4,000	179	0.22
NY cotton	$ 5.00	5,625	231	0.21
CMX copper	$ 2.50	2,995	219	0.18
NY WTI oil	$10.00	1,875	25	0.13
CMX gold	$10.00	2,425	30	0.12
S&P 500	$ 5.00	31,250	365	0.06

Box 7-1.

of the calculation of a Value Index on various international markets. It should be noted that the LME (London Metals Exchange) contracts are not true futures contracts, and the trading rules are somewhat idiosyncratic for short-term trading by those not familiar with the metals markets.

I prefer to trade no more than four markets at a time when day trading, but others might aim for more or less. The contracts cho-

International Futures Markets Average True Range Value Index
MAY 5, 1995

Market	Tick	Initial margin	13-day ATR	Value Index
LME aluminium	$ 2.50	2500	514	0.51
LME zinc	$ 2.50	1250	235	0.47
SFE BAB	$23.50	1000	15	0.35
SFE NCP	$10.00	500	16	0.32
SFE SPI	$ 2.50	1600	201	0.31
SFE 10-yr Bond	$74.00	2800	11	0.29
LME nickel	$ 6.00	4800	226	0.28
LIFFE gilt	£15.60	1646	18	0.17
LIFFE 3-month	£12.50	781	11	0.17
LIFFE Bund	DM25.00	4940	28	0.14
SIMEX Nikkei	Y500	1132800	309	0.14
LIFFE FT 100	£2.50	4690	248	0.13
HKFE Hang Seng	HK$50	63550	127	0.10

Box 7-2.

sen should have a Value Index above 0.30 and preferably be diversified. From the contracts in Box 7-1 I would choose CBoT soy oil, CBoT wheat, IMM DEM/USD, and IMM Eurodollar. Those markets would be traded for the following few days, until all positions were quit and/or other markets became more attractive.

In addition to good value, the markets chosen should be enjoying a surge. The markets which are attractive for short-term trading are those which might appear overbought or oversold on a daily basis. At this time we are discussing the strategic choice of a target market, so the principle behind the Woodes Rogers strategy can be used as guide. Recall that this principle was to use the synergy of three technical indicators over three time frames to target and trade the market with the best potential in accord with the resources and goals of your policy.

The markets which are my favored short-term trading targets are those which have surged to the top of the profitability table of the Woodes Rogers strategy. These are markets which are in the last stages of surge or collapse, and thus are extremely risky for further intermediate-term trading. In short-term trading, it is possible to make money on the last stage of a thrusting move, as well as on the resultant, often violent, reaction.

At this stage I should mention that the computer system on which the real-time signal is viewed should be chosen carefully. Some systems have limited technical analysis capabilities, and my research in Australia has been unable to locate a system which has the capability for "studies on studies." There is one system on which my tactical study of MACD on 21-period momentum can be programmed, but others available to me lacked this capability. Some systems have preprogrammed time periods, and you will see that I make use of variable time periods. By the time that you read this book, no doubt systems will have advanced in the professional field, but care should be taken that your preferred technical indicators are available.

Intraday Time Frame

I use two time frames for short-term trading, preferably different—if the computer system has the capability—from the relatively standard 5-minute and 1-hour periods used by many traders.

The simplest intraday time frame is 1 hour because all on-line systems have the ability to show hourly charts. However, it is my belief that the popularity of day trading has increased the use of systems based on the hour time frame to the extent that hourly moving averages might be a crowd-following indicator. I have chosen an intraday time frame that is one-fifth the time that the market trades in a 1-day session.

The pit trading hours for Chicago Board of Trade U.S. Treasury Bond futures are 7:20 A.M. to 2:00 P.M. Chicago time. The T-Bond futures contract trades 400 minutes daily, so my medium time frame is one-fifth of the daily session, or 80 minutes. On a number of real-time computer systems I can adjust the bar so that the data is then illustrated as an open/high/low/close over an 80-minute time period.

At this time the trader must decide what emphasis to place on trading outside normal trading hours. There has been a growth of computerized trading systems in recent years to extend trading to up to 24 hours a day globally. I believe that eventually all trading will occur off the trading floor through a global computer network, if society continues to allow the pace of technological growth which we have experienced in the 1990s. However, I can say from experience that activity in many markets after hours in the mid-1990s leaves much to be desired, and that lightly traded markets can be subject to manipulation. Accordingly it is my policy to trade outside normal pit hours *only* when it is absolutely necessary.

A professional T-Bond trader, however, is likely to view trading after hours on the computerized system in the London time zone and Tokyo time zone as just as natural as trading through the Chicago pits. It is a policy decision to define your trading hours.

The computer offers a quote on S&P 500 Index futures nearly 24 hours a day, but trading is concentrated in the normal daily session of 8:30 A.M. to 3:15 P.M. Chicago time, which is 405 minutes long. My medium time frame bar for S&P 500 Index futures is 81 minutes.

Most traders will decide to remain with the standard hourly bar, but if it is your decision to dare to be different, the medium time frame will have to be calculated for each market.

Once the medium time frame is chosen, a shorter period must be selected. My preferred period is simply one-fifth of the medium time frame. For instance the CBoT T-Bonds period of 80 minutes is simply reduced to 16 minutes short term. The S&P 500 medium frame of 81 minutes can also be reduced to 16 minutes. CBoT wheat, on the other hand, with a reduced pit time of 225 minutes, has a medium term of 45 minutes and short term of 9 minutes.

Exponential Moving Averages

Once the market and time frame have been established on the computer screen, studies can be added. In line with my previously expressed philosophy I simply introduce the 3/13-period exponential moving-average combination to each time frame. If I am seeking to buy, the exponential moving averages are on the price *high.* If I am seeking to sell, the exponential moving averages are on the price *low.*

The strategy is relatively simple. The medium-term 3/13 exponential moving-average crossover will indicate the action that one wishes to take in the shorter time frame. Assuming that one wishes to buy (the medium-term 3-period crossing up through the 13-period), one can use the 13-period calculated average price (on the high) as the buy stop. If no action is taken in that 9- to 16-minute period, then the next 13-period average is used.

Once a long position is taken, the basis of the exponential moving averages is changed to seek the selling signal, on the low price. The stop is then continually entered as the 13-period average or quit immediately should the medium-term time frame signal reverse.

In the same manner as any successful trading system, the decision process is relatively simple, allowing for the monitoring of more than one market. In fact I suggest that, subject to resources, more than one market be traded so that the temptation to anticipate the mathematical signals is lessened. As many professionals will attest, the computer screen's rapidly changing signals draw one like a moth to a flame, and at times the temptation to "jump the gun" on a signal can become almost overwhelming. I suggest that switching concentration by changing screens (or making a cup of coffee) can reduce temptation.

Money Management

It is just as important to have money management rules in short-term trading as it is in the strategic trading for longer periods. The principles are the same, but the parameters will change. Excitement seekers will have different criteria than my conservative personality allows, but even "gung ho" traders should try to limit losses so that they are able to make repeated attacks on the market.

I can only give my conservative opinion. The preferred time frame for a position to be held is 3 hours to 5 days. At least one contract is needed to be held overnight, so the initial margin will limit the position. My parameter is that capital of a minimum of 3 times initial margin be available for each contract willing to be held overnight. The exchange clearinghouse calculates initial margin on the basis of overnight risk, so even should an unexpected turn of events occur, any losing position should be able to be quit on the opening, with the loss limited approximately to initial margin. Larger traders will of course watch overnight markets with a view to taking defensive action, if necessary, before the normal trading markets open.

Trading with 3 times the initial margin should allow an initial trade of three contracts in the morning, or two if the conditions are not right until the afternoon. In the closing periods of the day the total position will be liquidated, or one contract held overnight.

My parameter for holding a contract overnight is that the position should be in profit to the extent of average true range of the medium-term time frame. We defined true range earlier, and some computer systems can calculate this in real time on the short time frames. Some, like FutureSource, have a similar measure referred to as "volatility" or "historic volatility." Basically the profit in the contract should at least be equivalent to the likely next adverse move within that time frame. This will not safeguard against sudden overnight movements, and only extreme excitement seekers should hold positions ahead of scheduled announcements.

The main risk management method is the combination time frame exponential moving averages, and the disciplined patience to stay out of the market when conditions are not right.

Examples

S&P 500 Futures

In mid-May 1995 the U.S. stock market was nervously overbought because of the constant rises without any reasonable reaction.

At 8:30 May 17 the 81-minute time frame 3/13-period exponential moving average June S&P 500 crossed to give the strategic sell indicator.

Midmorning the rally occurred, which allowed stops to be placed based on the 13-period average (then below the actual market). (As described under Henry Morgan tactics, I prefer to await a correction before entering the short-time-frame order.)

At 11:27 a sell order was placed to sell three June S&P 500 contracts on stop 528.65.

At 11:30 the order was filled at 528.30.

For the remainder of the day stops were entered based on the 13-period (16-minute time frame) *high.*

At 3:10 the position was quit at 528.05 because the profit was only marginal, and certainly less than the average true range.

Based on a relatively high retail brokerage rate of $50 per round turn, profit at $225 was little more than break-even.

At 8:30 May 18 the three-contract position was reentered on the opening at 526.60.

Throughout May 18 stops were continually entered based on the 13-period (16-minute time frame) *high.*

At 3:10 May 18 the price was trading at 519.10, which was sufficiently profitable for one contract to be held overnight (average true range 515 points). Two contracts were quit at 519.40 for a net profit of $7040.

At 8:30 on May 19 the market opened relatively unchanged with insufficient incentive to restore the three-contract position.

Throughout the morning stops were continually entered based on the 13-period (16-minute time frame) *high.*

By noon the entered stops moved close to the market.

From 12:30 to 1:18, the market moved as follows:

12:30	519.75
12:46	519.65
1:02	519.60
1:18	519.60

At 1:20 May 19 the 519.60 was triggered so that the remaining contract was quit at 519.90 for a net profit of $3300.

Total profit for 3 days was $10,565 on available funds of $93,750, which explains the attraction of short-term trading.

Wheat Futures

The high initial margin for S&P 500 Index futures means that many semi-professionals would have insufficient capital to trade with my conservative money management parameter. Agricultural futures contracts can be more attractive to traders with less capital. In May 1995 CBoT wheat futures could have been traded with an initial margin of $845, or three contracts for $2535. Consider the following sequence of events.

At the May 19 opening the medium-term moving averages indicated that a bought position in CBoT wheat July futures should be sought.

Stops were placed based on the 13-period (9-minute time frame) exponential moving average of the *high.*

At 10:30 May 19 three CBoT wheat July contracts were bought at $359\frac{2}{8}$ cents/bushel.

As is often the case with Chicago grain contracts the market became choppy, resulting in the stop (on the 13-period exponential moving average of the *low*) being touched at 11:54.

At 11:54 May 19 three contracts were sold at $360\frac{2}{8}$ cents/bushel with no profit/loss after brokerage.

The buy stops based on the 13-period (9-minute time frame) exponential moving average of the *high* then were reentered.

At 1:10 May 19 one contract could have been bought at $360\frac{2}{8}$ cents/bushel but the proximity to the close of the session suggested that the purchase be postponed to the opening on the following day.

At 9:30 May 22 three contracts were bought at $363\frac{6}{8}$ cents/bushel on a fast-moving opening.

Throughout May 22 stops were continually entered based on the 13-period (9-minute time frame) exponential moving average of the *low.*

Total position was quit at 366 cents/bushel on the close because there was insufficient profit to hold one contract overnight.

Net profit was $187.50 on available funds of $2535. The relatively miserable return was caused by my risk management parameter of not holding overnight, which missed half the move.

It would be misleading to give only highly profitable examples.

Nor have I given many examples of losses.

The examples I have shown are a minuscule illustration of short-term trading. Further more varied examples here are unlikely to bolster short-term profits, because short-term trading must be experienced, not learned.

The pirate who had to fight with a cutlass would need to practice with the unwieldy weapon before he was competent. The pistols had to be primed and loaded correctly, else they misfired. The pirates who survived had to be competent at close hand-to-hand combat, and learn from each battle experience.

Traders should study to become competent, and gain experience in less expensive markets, before trying their hand at the high-value, high-risk markets.

Hints for Scalpers

There are many books which give recommended methods for day traders and scalpers. I am not in favor of ad hoc trading, but there are many thousands of successful traders who would disagree with me. I will simply pass on a few hints which cost me quite a lot of money to learn, and which I hope that you will save money by heeding.

1. *Plan your trade; trade your plan.* I believe that a trading plan is just as necessary when day trading as it is in longer-term strategic position taking. Start the trading session with expectations that the market will move in a particular direction, and a plan to trade in that direction. A contingency plan should be formulated before the session commences, on the trading activity, if any, when the initial expectations are not met.

2. *Do not trade on impulse.* In a trading floor environment it is easy to be caught up in sentiment generated by other traders which does not necessarily agree with your trading plan. Even when alone watching a computer screen, one can become mesmerized by the tick-by-tick advance of the market into entering a nonplanned trade. Impulse trades have probably cost me more money than any other single factor.

3. *Practice relaxed concentration in undirected alertness.* The great mythologist Joseph Campbell told the story that in olden Japan a young man wishing to learn swordsmanship would be left by the master swordsman alone to do the chores around the dojo. From time to time the teacher would erupt from a hiding place to hit the student with a stick. After many days of this treatment the student would look for his master to spring from certain hiding places. This would do him no good because the sensei would wait until the expectation was centered on one direction, and then surprise the apprentice from another direction. Soon the bruised youth would realize that his only protection would be to stay alert for an attack from any direction. His protection would be in a perpetual state of undirected alertness, ever ready for a sudden attack and immediate response.

This hint is really a corollary of the first recommendation above. Do not raise your expectations that the market will follow a particular course so high that you fail to recognize that the market is reversing direction.

At times when you have been stopped out, be alert for the market to turn again, back in the original direction. Often a quick reentry after a minor reversal can be very profitable. If the reentry is delayed, the natural sentiment is to wait for another chance—which might not come until it is too late.

4. *Trade the long Elliot Waves.* Become aware of Elliot Waves in short-term trading. One does not need to be an expert in Elliot theory to look for waves 3 and 5 for the longest trend. Elliot theory should not run counter to your trading plan, but could provide the confidence to take a strong position.

5. *The first hour sets the tone.* The most important time for market entry is in the first hour of the trading session. This should be the time when your expectations are confirmed or not. More often than not, a change of trend established in the first hour will only be reversed by new information to the market. This is by no means certain, but, as Damon Runyon said, "The race is not always to the swift, nor the battle to the strong, but that's the way to bet."

Conclusion

I have tried to demonstrate throughout this book that, by using the past experience of others, you can formulate a trading system which will suit your own resources and goals. I have also tried to demonstrate that a speculator's life is not easy. It takes diligent application of the principles to achieve extended success. I hope that some day you will be able to share some of your experiences as a successful speculator with others.

Of course, assuming that you are successful you will need to take advice on tax minimization, so that you can hold on to the hard-won gains from the market.

You might recall that the privateer Woodes Rogers was held to be successful after he returned to England with treasure after circumnavigating the world. In fact the hazards of the legal profession and the East India Company proved more costly to Rogers than the perils of the voyage. After legal haggling between owners, officers, crew, and the profiteering East India Company, Rogers' share of the prizes was £1530, barely sufficient to cover the family debt of his three years at sea.

South Sea Bubble

Woodes Rogers might have had his revenge on those who diminished his rewards from the privateer treasure. In need of money, he wrote a book about the adventure, *A Cruising Voyage Around the World.* Together with William Dampier's journals, Rogers' book is thought to have inspired the investment in the South Sea Company. In 1720 the Company triggered the wave of speculation in the fledgling English stock market which became known as "the South Sea Bubble."

Woodes Rogers, who had become first governor of the Bahama islands, might have been indirectly responsible for the world's first recorded stock market speculative boom and bust.

Box 7-3.

One of Rogers' companions on his voyage was probably the most successful of the privateers. Dr. Thomas Dover, the city of Bristol's leading physician, guarded his investment in the owners' syndicate by assuming the role of medical chief for the voyage. The only owner present, he made himself chairman of the council of officers with a double vote in case of deadlock. Dover's actions in the long adventure endeared him to no one, but he ended up with a small fortune in invested shares, physician's salary, "storm money" as the nominal commander of the Guayaquil attack (which he opposed in council), and a bonus as chief captain of the galleon prize brought back to England (on which, as a nonseaman, he was merely a ranked passenger).

I can only say in conclusion that you now have the written hints to make your fortune from the markets. Might I suggest that you continue your education, with practical application, so that your privateering prizes are not lost to the pirates of bureaucracy.

Bibliography

Appel, G. *The Moving Average Convergence-Divergence Method:* Great Neck, N.Y., Signalert, 1979.

Bernstein, J. *Beyond the Investors Quotient:* New York, John Wiley & Sons, 1986.

Bernstein, J. *The Investor's Quotient:* New York, John Wiley & Sons, 1980.

Bernstein, J. *The Handbook of Commodity Cycles:* New York, John Wiley & Sons, 1980.

Cordingly, D., and J. Falconer. *Pirates—Fact and Fiction:* London, Collins & Brown, 1992.

Crapp, H. R. *Money Market Maths:* Sydney, Allen & Unwin, 1987.

Davidson, J. D., and W. Rees-Mogg. *Blood in the Streets:* London, Sidgwick & Jackson, 1988.

Douglas, M. *The Disciplined Trader:* New York, New York Institute of Finance, 1990.

Edwards, R. D., and J. McGee. *Technical Analysis of Stock Trends:* Boston, John McGee Inc., 1984.

Eng, W. F. *Technical Analysis of Stocks, Options & Futures:* Chicago, Probus Publishing, 1988.

Eng, W. F. *The Day Traders' Manual:* New York, John Wiley & Sons, 1993.

Fischer, R. *Fibonacci Applications and Strategies for Traders:* New York, John Wiley & Sons, 1993.

Frost, A. J., and R. Prechter. *Elliot Wave Principle:* New York, New Classics Library, 1981.

Gann, W. D. *The Truth of the Stock Tape:* Washington, Lambert-Gann Publishing Co. Inc., 1976.

Gann, W. D. *How to Make Profits in Commodities:* Washington, Lambert-Gann Publishing Co. Inc., 1976.

Gehm, F. *Commodity Market Money Management:* New York, John Wiley & Sons, 1983.

Gilmore, B. T. *Time and Price Analysis of Stocks and Commodities:* Melbourne, Bryce T. Gilmore & Associates, 1988.

Graham, B. *The Intelligent Investor:* New York, Harper & Row, 1973.

Hamilton, A. *The Financial Revolution:* New York, Macmillan Inc., 1986.

Huntley, H. E. *The Divine Proportion:* New York, Dover Publications, 1970.

Kaufman, P. J. *Commodity Trading Systems and Methods:* New York, John Wiley & Sons, 1978.

Kaufman, P. J. *Smarter Trading:* New York, McGraw-Hill, Inc., 1995.

Labuszewski, J., and J. Nyhoff. *Trading Financial Futures:* New York, John Wiley & Sons, 1988.

Le Bon, G. *The Crowd:* Atlanta, Cherokee Publishing Company, 1982.

Lefevre, E. *Reminiscences of a Stock Operator:* Greenville, S.C., Traders Press Inc., 1985.

Loosigan, A. *Foreign Exchange Futures:* Homewood, Ill., Dow-Jones Irwin, 1981.

Loosigan, A. *Interest Rate Futures:* Homewood, Ill., Dow-Jones Irwin, 1980.

Mitchell, D. *The Pirates:* London, Thames & Hudson, 1976.

Miyamoto, M. (trans. Nihin Services). *The Book of Five Rings:* New York, Bantam Books, 1992.

Mottram, R. H. *A History of Financial Speculation:* London, Chatto & Windus, 1929.

Murphy, J. J. *Technical Analysis of the Futures Markets:* New York, New York Institute of Finance, 1986.

Palgrave (ed.). *Dictionary of Political Economy:* London, McMillan, 1896.

Plummer, T. *Forecasting Financial Markets:* London, Kogan Page, 1990.

Powers, M., and D. J. Vogel. *Inside the Financial Futures Markets:* New York, John Wiley & Sons, 1981.

Rankin, H. F. *Golden Age of Piracy:* Williamsburg, Colonial Williamsburg, 1969.

Schumpeter, J. *Business Cycles:* Philadelphia, Porcupine Press, 1982.

Slatyer, C. W. *Australian Financial Futures Trading:* Sydney, Allen Unwin, 1985.

Slatyer, C. W., and E. Carew. *Forex—The Techniques of Foreign Exchange:* Sydney, Allen Unwin, 1989.

Slatyer, C. W., and E. Carew. *Trading Asia-Pacific Financial Futures Markets:* Sydney, Allen Unwin, 1993.

Sperandeo, V. *Trader Vic II: Principles of Professional Speculation:* New York, John Wiley & Sons, 1994.

Schwager, J. D. *Market Wizards:* New York, Harper Business, 1990.

Schwager, J. D. *The New Market Wizards:* New York, Harper Business, 1992.

Sun Tsu (trans. R. L. Wing). *The Art of Strategy:* New York, Doubleday, 1988.

Taylor, S. *Modelling Financial Time Series:* London, John Wiley & Sons, 1986.

Teweles, R. J., C. V. Harlow, and H. L. Stone. *The Commodity Futures Game: Who Wins? Who Loses? Why?:* New York, McGraw-Hill Inc., 1974.

Wilder, J. W. *New Concepts in Technical Trading Systems:* Greensboro, N.C., Trend Research, 1978.

Winston, A. *No Purchase, No Pay:* London, Eyre & Spotteswoode, 1970.

Index

ABOUT THE AUTHOR

Will Slatyer is an internationally recognized expert in the fields of stocks, commodities, interest rates, and foreign exchange. He travels the globe teaching his successful methods at traders' gatherings such as the Futures International Conference and Computrac Conferences. He has also been the keynote speaker at meetings of the Nippon Technical Analysts Association and Australian Technical Analysts Association. Slatyer served in the Australian Navy as a frogman, an experience that fueled his interest in naval history and the exploits of pirates. The author of three previous books on futures trading and foreign exchange, Slatyer lives in Manly, Australia.